"We so frequently think of the from lack of everything: money, self-esteem, dreams for the future, that it is good to be reminded that some folk had a different possibility. Martha's Vineyard offered the community another view of the world. These are serious folk with serious ideas for the future. They are not just sitting on the dock of the bay, as it were. Kevin Parham joins the group of young middle class writers who are flying on the wings of their future while holding tightly to their roots. *The Vineyard We Knew* is a totally wonderful look at a community that has been much too silent about its contribution and possibilities."

Nikki Giovanni—Poet, Author, and Educator

"*The Vineyard We Knew* is a series of vivid reflections of youthful summers. The writing is clear and concise, the stories are refreshing. These passionate memoirs, written in a fluid style, capture the appeal of the Vineyard. This is a book for people who have fond memories of their youth. I think it's a book with a broad appeal, from an emotive account of Parham's youth to his appreciation and love for Martha's Vineyard. Whenever he visits the Vineyard, he feels he is coming home. The reader will feel that way about *The Vineyard We Knew*."

Thomas Dresser—Author

"Parham's recollections give authentic testimony that for over 100 years—summer life on the Vineyard has been a family affair, a family experience, and a family tradition for generations of African Americans."

Bob Hayden—Historian, Author, and Educator

"Anyone wondering why African-Americans have come to Oak Bluffs generation after generation need only read Kevin Parham's *The Vineyard We Knew*. Parham's delightful recollections take the reader deep inside the wondrous and sometimes naughty adventures he shared with his young siblings, cousins and friends and lay bare the heart and soul of Oak Bluffs people.

And even when the journey is sometimes dark and haunting, and sometimes fraught with pain—especially from his grandmother's strap, Parham's captivating detail helps explain why people of color of all classes wanted (and still want) their children and grandchildren to come and enjoy a rare kind of freedom and adventure, and yes, character building."

Charlayne Hunter-Gault

Journalist, Author and grateful inhabitant of Oak Bluffs

The Vineyard
We Knew

The Vineyard We Knew

A RECOLLECTION OF SUMMERS
ON MARTHA'S VINEYARD

KEVIN PARHAM

Pria Publishing
Plymouth, Massachusetts

Pria Publishing
P.O. Box 1815
Sagamore Beach, MA 02562
www.priapublishing.com

Cover design by George Foster, fostercovers.com
Interior design by Dorie McClelland, springbookdesign.com
Edited by Kathy Grow, DoWriteEditing.com

Printed in the United States of America
First Printing 2014

Library of Congress Control Number: 2013923658

ISBN 978-0-9849485-0-5

Publisher's Cataloging-in-Publication data

Parham, Kevin Juan.
    The Vineyard we knew : a recollection of summers on Martha's Vineyard / Kevin Parham.
        p. cm.
        ISBN 978-0-9849485-0-5
        Includes bibliographical references.

1. Parham, Kevin Juan. 2. Martha's Vineyard (Mass.) -- Biography.
3. Adolescence -- Martha's Vineyard (Mass.). 4. Summer -- Martha's Vineyard (Mass.). 5. Martha's Vineyard (Mass.) -- Social life and customs. I. Title.

F72.M5 .P37 2014
974.4/94 -- dc23   2013923658

∽ Dedication ∽

*This book is dedicated to the memory of my mother, Beatrice,
and my grandmother, Caroline,
each of whom possessed a special love for the Vineyard.*

*And to the memory of Jacqueline Matthews-Thomas,
who left us too soon, but never failed to
make the trip each year to the island she treasured.*

*Lastly, this book is for all who have been touched
by the Vineyard experience,
and for those who have yet to be . . .*

Contents

Acknowledgments

Writing this book was not something I had planned to do. In fact, the idea began as a simple suggestion that, after having been nurtured with healthy doses of encouragement, grew and blossomed into a worthwhile endeavor that was a joy for me to have been part of. It is with heartfelt thanks that I acknowledge the following outstanding individuals for their selfless contribution of time, energy, and support throughout the entire writing process. All were instrumental in making this book possible.

To my wife, Olivia: your suggestion to embark on this project was the seed that germinated into what is now a completed book. I thank you for your unwavering support and for tolerating the "wee hours of the morning" flashes of insight that compelled me to jot down a thought—sometimes in total darkness—to capture a nugget I wanted to include in the manuscript. I sincerely appreciate your patience during the two-and-a-half years of constant writing, rewriting, and editing hundreds of incarnations of the story, along with listening to endless dissertations of bits and pieces of chapters until I felt the material "flowed" just right.

To my brother, Joseph G. Parham Jr. ("Chuck"): thanks so much for supporting me in this endeavor. I enjoyed reminiscing with you over lunch at the Harbor View Hotel in Edgartown, where we recounted years of summers on the Vineyard and exchanged stories that, had we not actually lived through them, would fall under the guise of "Truth is stranger than fiction."

A special thank-you goes out to my aunt, Mrs. Florence O. Guess ("Auntie"), whose incredible recall and memories of specific people, places, and things provided valuable insight that allowed me to convey parts of this story accurately, particularly events that occurred long before I was born or when I was too young to have remembered. Auntie, I am truly grateful for the time you spent with me to discuss fond memories, and how you graciously filled in the blanks about our family, each of whom played a crucial role in this story.

To my cousin Char Guess-Bardques: I thank you for our fun and spirited discussions over the phone. Your blithesome memories of our time in Oak Bluffs provided an abundance of material that helped to bring these experiences to light. I also want to say "thanks" for dancing me into the floor when you came to the Vineyard for Ma's memorial service in October 2008. (I'm still recuperating from that!) Have you ever considered being a contestant on Dancing with the Stars?

Sincere thanks go to my cousin Vincent Guess, not only for your generosity in accommodating my availability to interview you, but also for providing me with priceless family photos and vintage Steamship Authority schedules from 1958 and 1967. Vince, I appreciated your support and enthusiasm throughout the evolution of this project.

To Dick Whitney: I thank you for the use of your photos of the Jetties and the Flying Horses, which added a wonderful

Acknowledgments

visual dimension to this project. I am grateful for your generosity and support.

I would like to acknowledge the impeccable work of my editor, Kathy Grow, for taking what was once just another manuscript and making it sing! Kathy, you are the best! Thank you.

To my interior book designer, Dorie McClelland: many thanks for creatively formatting the book in a manner that is so pleasing to the eye.

George Foster, you are truly the master when it comes to cover design. I appreciated your artistry, patience, and willingness to incorporate my conceptual ideas into this project. Your professionalism made the process seem effortless!

To David Benoit: thanks for allowing the use of your composition Morning Sojourn to announce this book project. Your virtuosity was a key component for which I am eternally grateful.

I thank Selden Bacon for graciously providing the cover image of the *Islander* inbound to Vineyard Haven.

To Gerald Matthews Jr. ("G-Man"): thanks for your technical expertise and marketing savvy. You were there from the beginning, and I appreciated your support!

Sincere thanks go to Loraine and Charles Carter for their enthusiasm and kind words of encouragement.

And to Edwin Young: I thank you for your excellent videographer skills, creativity, and early support.

My gratitude also goes out to Frederic "Trader Fred" Mascolo for his assistance in this project. The timeless quote you provided by the late Henry Beetle Hough is priceless. No more appropriate words could have been used to conclude this book. Thanks, Fred!

Preface

Throughout my adult life, recollections from as far back as I can remember—memories of the summers I spent on Martha's Vineyard—have surfaced as spontaneous vignettes. Having now been released from the vaults of my subconscious, these Vineyard experiences have taken on a life of their own. Occurring more frequently and with astounding clarity, these stories have demanded that they be told.

Although I've often reminisced with my family about our time on the Vineyard, and shared these improvised anecdotes with friends, it wasn't until the summer of 2008, after the passing of my mother, Beatrice, that I decided to document my experiences.

As I began the tasks of searching inward and of seeking out the accounts of family and friends, I soon realized there was indeed a unique story to be told, from my perspective and from that of relatives with me at my grandmother's house in Oak Bluffs, about our childhood summer life on the island of Martha's Vineyard.

This book was made possible because of my family—those who have transitioned on, as well as those of us who still remain.

Each played an essential role in this story of the joys celebrated and the pain felt, the lessons learned, and everything else. These experiences served as the beginning, as well as an end, of a unique and wonderful journey—one truly our own.

Author's Note:

The accounts in this book are all true, and every effort was made to convey them as accurately as possible. Each one is based on the recollections of the author and of family members and friends. To protect the identity of certain individuals depicted therein, their names have been changed.

The Vineyard
We Knew

East Chop Lighthouse

Introduction

The island of Martha's Vineyard is a magical place filled with enchantment and wonder. For more than half a century, I have been under its whimsical spell—one that continues to lure me back year after year.

Just as a migrating bird is compelled to return to a specific geographic region each spring, I gravitate back to the Vineyard. I do this not only to reconnect to a time gone by, but also to reenergize my soul so I am inspired to reach the full potential of my life's purpose. This compulsion is not unlike the behavior of certain species of fish that instinctively swim upstream to spawn. Regardless of distance or the seemingly insurmountable odds against reaching their destination, they forge ahead with unrelenting determination.

Those who visit Martha's Vineyard for the first time often develop an irresistible urge to come back, an urge most people don't readily recognize, perhaps because it resides at the sub-conscious—or even the deeper molecular—level. Just as is true when one is addicted to a powerful drug, once you are hooked, you reach a point at which you can no longer do without it.

I have long since crossed that line of demarcation in my relationship with Martha's Vineyard.

Whether it's hanging out downtown in Oak Bluffs . . . taking an invigorating swim in the medicinal waters that surround the island . . . hiking endless trails meandering through forests, fields, and meadows . . . traversing hills that lead you to the shore . . . or simply sitting alone at a beach watching the sun slowly fade to a reddish pink hue, I faithfully immerse myself in these and many other treasures this island has provided countless times over the course of many years. I never grow tired of or bored by them, but, instead, am reborn each time. With gratitude, I acknowledge the wonderful blessings that God has given me, particularly the summers spent on Martha's Vineyard.

That journey began when I was less than a year old and continues to this day—over fifty years later. However, when I spent summers there as a child, my personal feelings for the Vineyard were far from euphoric; it was simply a place I was sent to each year. The irony was that most people counted the days leading up to going to Martha's Vineyard; I used to count them down to the day I would be picked up and taken back home. Now—older, wiser, and more appreciative of this gem of an island—I find that, each time I go there, it is as if it were for the first time. Now I become animated and full of excitement with renewed thoughts of and feelings about tomorrow's promise.

During one trip to the Vineyard, my wife, Olivia, made an astute observation, and it wasn't until she shared this observation with me while on the ferry that I became aware of how I reacted each time we drove to the Steamship Authority dock in Woods Hole or to the *Island Queen* in Falmouth Heights to board the boat. She had noticed that, each time, I proceeded to identify the same landmarks, points of interest, personal anecdotes, and historical relevance that had become an integral part of my experiences on the Vineyard.

With the exuberance one feels when doing something exciting for the very first time, I recalled those experiences with crystal clarity. My eyes sparkled with joy and enthusiasm as I mentioned this and recounted that, much like a child on Christmas morning, giddy with excitement about what Santa might have left under the tree. That exuberance has never waned.

Many accounts of personal experiences on Martha's Vineyard have been written over the years, each one unique and no more or less relevant than any other. This particular story is, of course, my account of our summers on the Vineyard at a time when the mundane was not necessarily a prelude to boredom, a time when the plain things in life had meaning, when simplicity had its place.

However, this is an atypical account compared to those documented from the perspective of affluence or travelogues, in which people of means flock to the Vineyard on private jets or massive pleasure boats to live the leisurely life of ostentatious opulence, vacationing at sprawling summer estates while undaunted by the existence of common folk—like my family.

For neither wealth nor social status was part of the equation when we were there. Thus, absent those attributes, this is a story about family, discipline, survival, tough love, respect, camaraderie, and self-discovery, played out under humble circumstances.

The Vineyard we came to know was viewed through a

completely different lens, in which the dominating factor in our resilience was the closeness we had as family. This closeness buoyed our spirits and triumphantly carried us through the trials and sometimes harsh realities of life on the island when we were young.

Many surmise that anyone who ever had a summer home on Martha's Vineyard must have been affluent or socially connected to people with power and influence. But, in our case, nothing could have been further from the truth. While my grandmother once owned a modest, unheated, two-bedroom cottage on the Vineyard, it is also worth noting that it was neither her second nor third house; it was her only house, acquired at a time when she was fortunate to have been able to take advantage of an opportunity. That old, rickety summer house in Oak Bluffs served as one of the most influential anchors in my Vineyard life's story.

If that house still existed today and could talk, it would have much to say.

Town Beach at Oak Bluffs Wharf
Back Row, l-r: Ma, Joanne, Vincent, Auntie, and Carmella
Front Row: Family friend, Chuck, and Charlene

Chapter 1

Beginnings

*M*y siblings and I grew up in West Medford, Massachusetts, a close-knit African American community a few miles northwest of Boston. Like most kids, we eagerly looked forward to getting out of school for the summer because that was the time we got to do what we wanted. Our only challenge was to decide what to do on a particular day, and sometimes we took the entire day to make a decision. Should we hang out at Dugger Park or go to the Community Center? How about swimming at Sandy Beach or fishing from the banks of the Mystic Lakes? Perhaps we could play a game of baseball or football at one of the fields in the neighborhood. The possibilities were endless, and we had the whole summer ahead of us. Right?

Not so fast.

Soon after the final bell rang at the end of the school year, my mother—a forthright woman of medium build with a pretty round face and big brown eyes—packed our bags for the annual summer-long trip to our grandmother's on Martha's Vineyard.

As a child, I could not fathom why Ma sent us there; now that I am an adult, there is no question as to the reason why.

My family's visits to Martha's Vineyard began when my mother, Beatrice, and her siblings—Florence, Harry, and Lawrence Gamble—were brought to the island as teenagers by their mother, Carrie, in the late 1930s. They lived on Munroe Street in Roxbury, Massachusetts, just off Humboldt Avenue and not far from the tiny "upper-class" black section of town known as Sugar Hill. My grandmother looked forward to getting her children temporarily away from the city, where the mean streets could be unforgiving, even for a modest family such as theirs. They made the trip to the Vineyard each year, and over time, developed a unique love for the place—one that remained strong for over three-quarters of a century.

My mother's younger brother, Lawrence, had been seduced by the night life in Boston, and he enjoyed the spoils inherent in that lifestyle. Through a chance encounter while patronizing a local nightclub one evening, Uncle Lawrence befriended a then-unknown but charismatic young man named Malcolm Little, who happened to be staying with a sister at the time. Lawrence and Malcolm occasionally hung out together, and, when they weren't running the streets, they sometimes ended up at my grandmother's house. Malcolm conducted himself with the utmost courtesy and respect in the presence of my grandmother and her daughters each time he visited their home.

Two years later, Malcolm moved from Boston to Harlem, where he embarked on a tumultuous journey down a road that led to a life of crime for which he was sent back to Boston and incarcerated. While in prison, Malcolm made constructive use of his time by reading every book he could get his hands on; his insatiable appetite for learning turned him into a self-educated man.

When he was released from prison six years later, Malcolm had been completely transformed. He had discovered a path to enlightenment and redemption, and ultimately went on to become one of the most articulate and outspoken advocates for black people in the United States. For twelve years hence, Malcolm Little emblazoned his mark on history and fulfilled his destiny as a minister in the Nation of Islam under the name of Malcolm X. It is believed Malcolm X was one among many notable individuals to have visited Martha's Vineyard.

In the summer of 1955, when I was ten months old, my mother first brought me to Oak Bluffs, one of six small towns on the island of Martha's Vineyard. Back then, my family—Ma; my sister, Joanne; my brother, Chuck; and I—traveled by train from South Station in Boston to get to the ferry in Woods Hole.

While living in Medford, my mother—divorced with three children—had to search for any employment she could find to support our family. At one time, she worked at Raytheon Electronics, where she soldered circuit boards on an assembly line. That particular job lacked stability, and the income she earned was inconsistent due to the frequent layoffs and callbacks characteristic of that type of work. A few years later, her perseverance paid off when she secured a job with the Commonwealth of Massachusetts working as an attendant on the third shift at

Ma and Kevin

the Walter E. Fernald State School, a place that housed individuals afflicted with mental disabilities.

A dedicated and hardworking woman, she did her best to provide for us, even if it meant she personally had to do without. Because of her determination to stick to a budget, she always managed to put a few dollars away from each paycheck. Ma never allowed herself to be defined by material possessions, for, with unrelenting discipline, she followed strict fiscal principles in order to make ends meet. She went to great lengths to teach us the importance of "paying yourself first" and "living below your means" if we were to ever have anything in this life.

My mother was an introvert by nature, unassuming and with a quiet temperament, but all hell broke loose when she was driven to the edge, for she was quick-witted, and even sarcastic at times, because of her determination to tell it like it was.

And Ma was very protective of her children, which explains why I ended up on Martha's Vineyard.

To ensure that my brother, sister, and I were properly cared for while we were out of school and our mother was at work, we stayed with our grandmother on the Vineyard every summer from June until Labor Day.

My mother's sister, Florence, whom we called "Auntie," was an attractive woman of medium build with a rich brown

Uncle John, Charlene, and Auntie

complexion and flowing, dark brown hair. She was married, had two children, and lived in Boston. Auntie worked as a hairdresser at a local beauty salon, and she enjoyed the social interaction that came with the job. My aunt wore fashionable clothes and attended various events around the city whenever she could, for she was an excellent dancer, had an outgoing personality, and loved to have a good time with family and friends.

My aunt's husband, John Guess, was a tall, boisterous, fair-skinned man from Louisville, Kentucky, who worked at the General Electric plant. Uncle John had a colorful personality, and the timbre of his voice made him sound as if he were yelling at you when he spoke. One of his passions was playing the trumpet, and he spent many hours at home in the living room blowing to Louie Armstrong's or Miles Davis's albums on the record player.

Their two children, Charlene and Vincent, and their adopted niece, Carmella, came to the island for the summer, too, which meant that all of us cousins were together under the care of our grandmother, Carrie White.

During the 1950s and '60s, Martha's Vineyard had not yet become the popular vacation destination it is today. Located seven miles off the coast of Cape Cod, the island was so remote back then, it could just as easily have been a thousand miles away. In those days, you could drive down to the boat, purchase your tickets, and get your car on board immediately; advance reservations were not necessary because there were no standby lines, no crowds, and hardly ever any hassles. The lifestyle was laid back, and people you encountered were always friendly and willing to help out whether you were looking for information or just needed a hand.

Ma and Cool

The month of June had arrived, and, once again, we found ourselves preparing to leave for the Vineyard. But, this time, we were going to be riding in a car driven by my stepfather, John Henry Hammonds, whom we nicknamed "Cool" because he was, or so he thought.

Cool was a quiet, robust man with a dark complexion and balding head. Born and raised in Columbus, Georgia, he moved to Massachusetts in the 1950s and met my mother at Raytheon Electronics, where he worked as an electrical tester. In 1959, Cool and my mother were married, and, shortly thereafter, my younger sister, Deirdre, was born.

John Henry was a habitual smoker of Pall Mall and Philip Morris cigarettes, and he enjoyed the taste of a cold beer as well as a nip from Old Crow whiskey. Cool was the type who stayed in the background, leaning against the kitchen counter, propped up on his elbows, while quietly listening to what was being discussed. If so inclined, he would interject his opinion into the conversation and then abruptly disappear from the room before you had a chance to respond.

My stepfather, being from the South, loved his southern food. He ate a steady diet of collard greens, black-eyed peas and rice, chitterlings, pigs' feet, pig ears, oxtails, okra, and corn bread. At dinnertime, Cool sat at the kitchen table with a bottle of Tabasco sauce or Frank's Red Hot Sauce within his reach. Only a few drops of either of these condiments made the food taste so hot, he would sweat profusely and had to wipe his brow with a handkerchief while he ate. I found it curious that he actually enjoyed his meals under such circumstances.

>>>

It was a glorious Saturday morning when we left for the Vineyard, and, as my stepfather's white '57 Buick wagon—loaded down with the family, luggage, and anything else that could be crammed into it—cruised down the expressway, a warm, humid breeze blended with the exhaust fumes and circulated through the open car windows. The seventy-three-mile trip to Cape Cod took about two hours to complete, and, by the time we arrived in Woods Hole, we were soaked in perspiration from sitting on the worn vinyl seats that absorbed the warmth from the sun.

"We've finally made it!" my mother said with a smile as the car made its way down the hill to the staging area. The ferry *Islander* was docked at the slip, and my stepfather parked behind a line of vehicles about to board. The rest of us waited in the station wagon while he walked into the ticket office to get the passenger tickets and boarding pass for the car.

"Ma, can we get out of the car now?" Chuck asked.

"It's too dangerous for you to play in this parking lot. We'll be getting on the boat soon, so just be patient. You'll be able to go up to the deck and look at the view then," she said.

Less than fifteen minutes later, we were on the ferry making our way from the freight deck to the upper level. The strong odor of diesel fuel choked us, and a loud rumble from the boat's engines made it difficult to hear as we climbed the metal stairs. Because my young mind was incapable of grasping the concepts of physics, I was amazed at how this big hunk of steel, weighed down by cars, trucks, and passengers, was able to stay afloat.

After reaching the upper deck of the vessel, we found ourselves at the snack bar, where the smell of hot dogs, hamburgers, and a variety of other foods masked the irritating fumes from downstairs where the vehicles were parked. Other passengers in the snack bar engaged in lively conversation as they consumed sandwiches, chips, candy, ice cream, and sodas.

Moments later, we stepped through a narrow door to the outside deck, where rows of dark green plastic chairs were lined up next to one another, unoccupied. The view overlooking Vineyard Sound and the Elizabeth Islands was spectacular. A short blast of the horn signaled our departure as the *Islander* slowly pulled away from the dock. Almost immediately, she made a hard left turn in front of a red buoy, keeping her away from shallow water where dangerous rocks were hidden below the surface. After passing between a pair of green and red markers a short distance away, she made another left turn, pointing the ferry toward Martha's Vineyard.

The Nobska Point Lighthouse stood high on a hill to the left, intermittently flashing a white beacon as we sailed by. Looking off in the distance from the bow of the boat, the tips of West Chop and East Chop appeared on the horizon, gradually increasing in size and clarity as we drew closer to the island.

The sunlight reflected off the water and created a shimmering display as we sailed toward the Vineyard. White puffy clouds floated against a deep blue sky, and a flag on a pole fluttered aimlessly in the stiff ocean breeze. Seagulls glided effortlessly on the wind as they followed the ferry in search of food passengers tossed to them, and some of the fearless birds dove into the water to snatch fish churned up by the rotating propellers. We passed numerous pleasure boats during the trip across.

I remember developing an affinity for boats at an early age, and often wondered what it would feel like to get behind the wheel of one and pilot it myself. The forty-five minute excursion to the island was rejuvenating.

Before long, the ferry entered Vineyard Haven Harbor, our pending arrival announced by the sound of a long blast from its air horn, startling us as it reverberated through our bodies and made us cover our ears with our hands to mute the noise. We scurried down the stairs to the car, noticing that the ferry's engines had fallen silent as the stout vessel slowly coasted its way to the pier. Crew members stood on the freight deck and waited to begin the task of manually opening two large steel doors through which the vehicles would soon disembark.

The *Islander* entered the slip, and we again heard the roar of its engines as they displaced the ocean water to slow the boat down, which made it bounce off the pilings and jerk us forward as it settled in to be secured to the dock. The signal was given, and we drove off the ferry and headed to our grandmother's house, three miles away.

While making our way down Beach Road and over the draw-bridge toward Oak Bluffs, familiar sights indicative of island life unfolded before us. To the left, men with fly rods were fishing from a jetty in the harbor; off to the right, small cottages sat nestled in thick underbrush some distance from the road. Salt-water and freshwater ponds, sprinkled with lilies and a variety of aquatic wildlife, were visible from the car as we whisked by. Native flowers, plants, and trees grew in abundance as far as the eye could see, and a sweet fragrance filled the air, all truly beautiful to behold.

Within minutes, we turned on to Pacific Avenue and con-tinued up the street to where the elementary school next to my grandmother's house and the Oak Grove Cemetery across the street came into view. At that point, we knew we had arrived. As our car entered the grassy driveway, Nana stepped out of the house to greet us.

"Well, I see that you made it down safely. How was your trip?" she asked.

"The trip was fine," my mother replied.

"Hi, Nana!" we yelled in unison.

"Hello, children; welcome to the island. Your cousins, Char-lene, Vincent, and Carmella, will be down later today. In the meantime, you can bring your suitcases into the house," she said.

Each time we were brought to the island for the summer, my

mother and stepfather stayed just long enough to get us settled, usually a day or two. And, every year, the same fear and apprehension overwhelmed me as I thought about being separated from my mother for three long months.

Auntie and Uncle John arrived that evening with my cousins, completing the transfer of us grandkids to the island for our yearly Vineyard visit. With the family's arrival now complete, our grandmother's house turned into a place bustling with chaotic activity well into the night.

The adults hung out in the kitchen, engaging in spirited discussions about life while partaking in libations. We kids entertained each other with stories, teasing, and laughter as we bounced off the walls in the den. It was close to midnight when the excitement finally reached its crescendo, and soon we cousins ended up falling asleep in chairs, on the couch, sprawled out on the floor, or wherever we happened to be.

Our summers on the Vineyard always began in this fashion, but, once our parents left the island early the next morning, we knew our lives would be much different from what we were used to back home.

48 Pacific Avenue, Oak Bluffs Massachusetts

Chapter 2

Morning

*T*he sun slowly awakened, and, as it began its ascent into the eastern sky, golden rays of light danced upon droplets of morning dew. Dawn was beckoning on the Vineyard, and a faint, intermittent drone from a foghorn moaned in the distance as it cut through the misty air on a cool June morning.

Loud clucks and cackles drifted from a chicken coop across the schoolyard where roosters welcomed the new day with vigor, attempting to out-crow each other as if they were competing in a contest. Seagulls squawked with aggression while circling overhead in search of sustenance, and the colorful morning glories, snaked up a trellis made from ordinary white string in my grandmother's garden, opened their fragrant blue, purple, and white petals in splendor.

The robust aroma of freshly percolated coffee displaced the musty air as it wafted to the second floor of the old, rickety two-bedroom summer home. As I emerged from slumber, I felt the dampness of mildew permeate the room, sending a shiver up my spine.

Upon rising, I hastened my morning ritual because of remnants of the cool night; I wanted to get dressed and go downstairs without delay. The walk down those old, dimly lit, wooden stairs leading to the small kitchen was made with apprehension because the creaking noises every time I stepped on them scared me. The result of making it to the bottom of those stairs each morning was always consistent. I knew I would find my grandmother, Carrie, sitting at the kitchen table playing Solitaire in front of an old cast-iron stove.

When Nana ended her card game, she would say,

"Go wash up so you can have your breakfast."

"Okay," I would respond, and make my way to the tiny bathroom situated just off the den on the first floor.

Because of constant plumbing problems, running water wasn't always available at the house. To address this issue, we would walk over to the graveyard across the street, use its faucets, and bring back buckets of water for personal hygiene, cleaning, and cooking.

As I stared at my reflection in the small round mirror over the sink, I thought about how those trips to the graveyard under the cover of darkness were a regular occurrence for my siblings, cousins, and me. The buckets of water were heavy, and hauling them back to the house was always a challenge, for we were just kids. We did our best not to spill any of the precious liquid cargo. When we got back to the house after each trip, we emptied the contents into a big pot on the stove, and Nana boiled the impurities out of the water for future use.

Refocusing my attention on the task at hand, I gingerly washed my face with the cold water and began to anticipate the food that awaited my arrival at the breakfast table. One by one—as if on cue—my sister, brother, and cousins also made their way downstairs to the kitchen to partake in the morning meal.

We crowded around an old wooden table, snugly pushed against the wall and covered by a dull red-and-white checkered tablecloth, as a hearty breakfast of scrambled eggs, bacon, and grits was served. If any of us had even the slightest inclination to say we were not hungry, or, for some reason, didn't want to eat what was being served for that particular meal, we would be making a grave mistake.

Once in a while—if we were lucky—we'd get a temporary reprieve thanks to my cousins' pet collie, Champ. This dog had a friendly temperament and was the spitting image of the famous TV dog, Lassie. He was more than willing to consume almost anything we managed to sneak to him beyond the watchful eye of our grandmother. Champ was a well-behaved canine whose simple needs were met by being fed, watered, and occasionally having ticks hiding beneath his thick coat of fur removed by Uncle John, who burned them off with a lit cigarette.

This morning, Champ was no help. "Finish your grits!" Nana said to Chuck.

"But, Nana, I don't want to eat the grits," he said.

"Well, you'll just sit there until you do," retorted Nana, in her stern, no-nonsense manner. The only one of us still sitting at the table, my brother repositioned the food on his plate and reluctantly gobbled down the cold, hardening grits that gagged him every time he attempted to swallow.

After breakfast, we were always instructed to go outside and play, except if it was raining. When it rained, our only means of escape from the wet, musty conditions inside the house disappeared. In fact, we grandkids looked forward to getting out of the house to dry off in the warmth of the summer sun.

Because our grandmother's house was small, it couldn't accommodate many people at once, and it wasn't unusual to find anywhere from five to eight children and a dog staying there at any time. Whenever relatives or friends came down to stay with us, the cramped accommodations made us feel like sardines tightly packed into a can.

Another reason we spent so much time outside was because our grandmother, a strict disciplinarian from the "old school," believed that children should be seen and not heard, particularly in the presence of adults. When any of her friends stopped by the house for a visit, we were immediately ushered from the area where the adults engaged in their conversations.

Our existence on the island was a humble one, and things were in a constant state of disrepair at the house. I vividly remember the summer when the kitchen walls almost collapsed after the floor started to buckle and the ceiling began to sag. Fortunately, Nana knew a gentleman named Mr. Wigglesworth, a stocky old man, who, because of his propensity to mumble to himself, appeared to be engaged in an ongoing conversation regardless of whether anyone was around him or not. His area of expertise happened to be structural engineering, and he fixed the problem by reinforcing the walls and ceiling, which prevented the roof from caving in.

There were many times when we had to do without some of the basic necessities of life. No running water? Head for the cemetery. Electricity off? Get a flashlight or light a candle. No oil for the stove? Fire up the barbeque grill in the backyard. At that time, I used to think the term "creature comforts" referred to things only people of wealth could afford, so it made perfect sense that we didn't have any of those things.

"You kids can go outside now, but stay close to the house so I can keep an eye on you," Nana said.

The worn-out screen door to the kitchen swung open as we left the house, and an irritating screeching sound emanated from the rusty spring as the door snapped back with a *crack*.

Once outside, we saw that the morning fog was rapidly losing the battle with the intense sunlight. It quickly dissipated, prompting the locusts to buzz loudly—an early indicator of how hot this day would be. On the outer perimeter of the yard, yellow daffodils gently swayed in the breeze. Wild flora and grasses, mimicking a sea of green, gold, and brown, were visible across the yard and up the gentle slope leading to the street.

Because I was younger than my brother, sister, and cousins, they had more latitude than I did as to how far they could wander away from the house. Consequently, my options were limited.

My favorite place to play was in the schoolyard next door. This fairly large, unkempt space—composed of sand, rocks, weeds, pieces of broken glass, and a few bottle caps thrown in for good measure—was where my imagination took flight. Of course, there were the usual things you would expect to find in a school playground, including a set of swings, monkey bars, and a seesaw, but those were not the things I was drawn to.

In my mind's eye, the vast area of sand in the playground had become an ocean of bluish green water, complete with waves and whitecaps. And, as the captain of my very own ferryboat—nothing more than an old block of discarded wood—I pushed this vessel of make-believe through the hot sand with my bare hands. For hours, I reenacted the trips of the real ferries traveling from Woods Hole to Martha's Vineyard without ever noticing the stifling heat as the summer sun blazed down upon me.

The sound of our grandmother's high-pitched, melodic voice suddenly jarred me back to reality.

"Kevin, Chucky, Charlene, Vincent, come home! It's time to eat."

"Yes, Nana," I answered, as my brother and cousins also scampered back to the house in response to her call. Joanne and Carmella were already sitting at the table by the time we got there.

"What's for lunch, Nana?" Vincent asked.

"Peanut butter and jelly sandwiches," she said.

We all smiled and nodded in appreciation of what was being served. The white bread used to make the sandwiches wasn't just any white bread, and, as Chuck and I looked at each other and grinned, we began reciting the commercial advertisement for this particular brand: "That's what ahhh said . . . Bunny Bread!"

We began eating our sandwiches, each in our own unique ways. I liked to cut mine in half diagonally; two preferred eating theirs whole; two more liked quarter pieces; and the other ate the crust around the outside of the sandwich first. No matter how you ate it, there was no escaping the stick-to-the-roof-of-your-mouth sensation you got with each successive bite, which *had* to be washed down with an ice-cold glass of ZaRex—a sweet, sticky syrup diluted in water.

Morning

When lunch was over, we cleared off the table and brought the crumb-filled, peanut butter and jelly–stained plates to the sink to be washed. Peering into the drain, I noticed the pipe was missing under the sink. Normally, a drain is dark when you look down into it, but, at our house, the light poured not only through the drain, but also through a hole in the kitchen floor, exposing the bare ground underneath. I surmised that this was just another example of the plumbing problems we had to deal with, but, in this instance, the problem was that there was no plumbing.

The rising temperature from the afternoon sun engulfed the house like flames in a woodstove, and the gray shingles on the roof appeared to melt as black tar adhesive bubbled up in the intense heat. With hopes of luring the slightest breeze into the house, the front door leading to the screened-in porch and the kitchen door at the back of the house were simultaneously left ajar.

We often retreated to the front porch to lay low when it was too hot outside, and there was never a lack of conversation or playful interaction among us grandchildren during the many hours spent there. The outside entrance to the porch was never used because the stairs were dilapidated and too dangerous to walk on, so we always went through the house to get to the front porch. The route was the same each time—kitchen, den, living room, porch.

The living room had a strange ambience. It was dimly lit, regardless of the time of day, and passing through it always felt as if you were walking through a tunnel. Dark curtains hung loosely from two windows facing each other on either side of the room, and an old hand-crank phonograph player sat inconspicuously in the corner. Positioned against the opposite wall was a dusty black-and-white television set that displayed snowy images when it was turned on. Something peculiar about that room made you quicken your pace as you went through it, eager to reach the comforting daylight radiating from the porch.

Facing east, the front porch was in the shade during the hottest part of the day and provided a respite from the unforgiving sun. A white wicker sofa with dingy cushions, as well as several old armchairs, provided us with places to sit and doubled as makeshift props for our youthful antics.

Directly adjacent to the porch was a narrow dirt path to the schoolyard, the preferred route for neighbors heading into town. In the distance, a tall, thin man wearing blue jeans, a white long-sleeved shirt, sneakers, and a straw hat slowly made his way down the path toward us. As he got closer, we could see the stoic face and rigid demeanor that gave him the appearance of being in a trance. He placed one foot in front of the other in a mechanical fashion that somehow propelled him forward. You could see his cocoa brown skin was blotched and discolored as he trudged past us.

"Hello, Scarface," Charlene said, with a wave of her hand. Without slowing down or stopping, Scarface slightly turned his head toward her and responded with a low, expressionless moan, then continued his journey down the dusty path.

"What's wrong with him?" I asked.

"I think he has a skin disease," Charlene said.

"He's slow," Joanne said.

"He's not slow; he's mental," Vincent said, with cold

conviction. "All he does is traipse around all day without uttering two words to anyone. Now wouldn't you call that being crazy?"

Scarface was an unusual character. He stayed with relatives down the street and was more or less a fixture in the neighborhood. A harmless soul, he kept to himself while aimlessly roaming around, though he occasionally yelled out obscenities at us as he walked past the house. Watching him was similar to watching a farm animal wander around a barnyard.

After we played countless hands of Fish and War and read many adventures of comic book superheroes, shadows appeared out of nowhere as dusk rapidly fell upon us. It was close to suppertime, and Nana was in the kitchen preparing the evening meal while listening to a cheap, tinny-sounding transistor radio she kept on the cupboard. A large metal pot was boiling on the stove, but what it contained was a mystery because the cover tightly sealed it.

"What's in the pot, Nana?" I inquired.

"Layovers," she said. "Layovers to catch meddlers."

I supposed that was Nana's way of avoiding the question, so I decided to find out for myself. I approached the pot and reached over to lift the cover, when Nana's small but strong hand intercepted mine with a quick, cobralike smack.

"Oh, no you don't," she scolded. "You'll see what it is when you eat."

And that was the conundrum that faced us every time we sat down for a meal.

For, if there was anything you could be sure of when it came time to eat at Nana's house, it was that you never knew what would be placed before you for your eating pleasure—or displeasure, depending on your perspective. An example of this uncertainty involved a goat from a local farm that ended up on our dinner table as the main course one evening.

During the previous week, Uncle John had taken us to an up-island farm where an acquaintance of his worked. This mild-mannered gentleman gave us a tour of the farm and allowed us to run around and play with some of the animals there. In addition to those one would find on a typical New England farm, an old goat also was confined to a pen enclosed with chicken wire. Every day that week, we went up to the farm to see that lonely goat and to feed it blades of grass and hay; we even got to pet it while it ate.

As it turned out, our feeding sessions were just a prelude to the goat's demise; it had developed an illness of some sort and had to be put down. Unbeknown to us, after fattening up this doomed creature, Uncle John and his friend slaughtered the poor thing and brought some of the goat meat back to our grandmother's house to be cleaned, seasoned, and cooked.

We all sat around the dinner table that evening and found ourselves staring at some form of meat about to be served; however, even I knew enough to know it wasn't beef, chicken, fish, or pork. Only after the meal was over were we told that what we had eaten was our newly adopted pet, Billie the Goat. For several days afterward, just the *thought* of eating made me sick to my stomach.

Morning

Our grandmother's culinary talents were diverse; she was always able to whip something up from little or nothing. She made the world's best coleslaw from her own secret recipe—one others attempted to replicate—but, for some reason, their efforts never quite measured up.

Throughout the school year, Nana worked as an assistant cook at the Dexter School in Brookline, Massachusetts, the private school President John F. Kennedy attended through the fourth grade, along with his older brother, Joseph P. Kennedy Jr., before moving to New York with their family.

During the summer months, our grandmother held a job as a cook for the Gerrishes, an affluent Jewish family from New York that vacationed on the Vineyard each year. Every afternoon around 3:30, a dark blue, chauffeured limousine arrived at the house to pick Nana up and take her to an estate overlooking Vineyard Haven Harbor in East Chop, where she prepared dinner for their family.

The Gerrishes' residence was a quaint, gable-style green and white house on the water's edge, with accoutrements including a garage, private beach, and dock. While Nana was at work, my sister, Joanne—the oldest grandchild—was responsible for watching the rest of us. After completing her shift, Nana was dropped off at the house around 10:00 p.m., and we always anticipated her return home with excitement because sometimes she would surprise us with remnants of leftover food or desserts from the meal she had prepared that evening. The welcome sight of headlights turning into the driveway heightened our hopes that a sweet treat was forthcoming!

One night, we took our usual places at the dinner table and found a set of old, porcelain soup bowls with chips and hairline cracks, clearly reflecting many years of meals long past. Nana removed the lid from the pot, and, with a ladle, quickly scooped up servings of what appeared to be some kind of soup. But a closer examination revealed something much more profound. Immersed in the broth, along with ingredients you would expect to find in your typical soup, were fish heads floating around in the bowl, their eyes staring up at us.

"What's this?" Chuck asked.

"Seafood stew," Joanne said.

"It looks more like fish-head stew, and I'm not eating it!"

"Me neither!" Vincent said.

I felt myself on the verge of nausea.

It was one thing for one of us to try to avoid eating something we did not like, but an all-out revolt staged by her grandchildren would never be tolerated.

"You all are going to eat your food—even if I have to personally shove it down your throats," Nana said. And she was true to her word.

Even Champ, the pet dog, always sitting patiently on the floor next to the table with hopes of receiving a morsel of food, was nowhere to be seen. Nana glanced at the strap hanging on the wall and casually positioned herself next to it, just in case we needed any additional coaxing. That move was enough to end the standoff at the dinner table, and, reluctantly, we conceded defeat and began eating the stew.

During the agonizing process of force-feeding ourselves, we tried our best to navigate around the fish heads playing hide-and-seek as they bobbed up and down in our bowls. The stew tasted like a concoction laced with cod liver oil and castor oil. Each spoonful was more pungent than the last, and all of us gagged on the food. As I sat there, I began to feel sick and broke out in a cold sweat. My stomach was doing flips—similar to the action of clothes tumbling in a dryer—and my skin turned cold and clammy.

After consuming what had to be the most disgusting meal ever served, we bolted from the small kitchen that reeked of boiled fish and went out to the yard to plop ourselves down in a chair or lie down on the bench. In a desperate attempt to cleanse our taste buds and soothe our nauseated stomachs, we breathed in the fresh air and looked around for anything to suck on—a strip of gum, a piece of candy, a mint, fruit; at that point, even a small rock would have sufficed to quell the sickening aftertaste of the fish-head stew.

"I can't believe she made us eat that shit!" Carmella said.

"Yeah, it was pretty nasty," Chuck said.

"Next time she tries to serve me any of that stuff, I'm going to refuse to eat it," Vincent claimed.

"Sure, and you'll get your ass kicked by Nana," Carmella said, with a smirk.

"No, I won't. I'll simply reason with her."

"Reason with whom?"

"Nana."

"In your dreams, buddy; you know there's no reasoning with Nana."

"Vincent, Carmella's right. But, then again, you'd probably get away with it. We *all* know that Nana is easier on you and Charlene because she lives with you in the winter," Chuck said.

"She might live with us, but there's no way she's easier on us.

Carrie doesn't take any crap from anyone—not even from my mother and father," Charlene said.

"Just about everyone on the island knows that Nana doesn't take any mess. I saw her get in a man's face one day and threaten to knock him out," I said.

"Nana has always been feisty, but that's Nana," Joanne said.

Our spirited discussion was interrupted by the sound of an old, noisy pickup truck sputtering down the street as it approached the house.

"Oh, no. Is it who I think it is?" Vincent asked.

The truck turned into the driveway and rolled toward us.

"Yup, it's him," I said.

As the truck came to a stop in front of where we were sitting, a scruffy-looking, brown-skinned man with chiseled features and jet black hair got out, wearing rubber boots, a raincoat, and a baseball cap. It was Tony, the fishman, an acquaintance of our grandmother's whose appearance at the house was our worst nightmare.

Tony was a Wampanoag Indian, and he stopped by every so often to give Nana some of the excess fish he had caught in Menemsha. The strong odor from his most recent catch attracted a swarm of flies, causing them to buzz frantically around the truck.

"Hi, kids. Is your grandmother home?" he asked.

We wanted to tell him she wasn't home, but we knew what the result of that would be.

"Hello, Tony. Nana's in the house," Joanne told him.

"Good. I've got plenty of fresh codfish and bluefish to give to her."

Oh, my God, I thought. *We'll be eating fish-head stew for the rest of our lives.*

Morning

Tony dropped off two bucketfuls of the slimy, stinking fish and left the house just as quickly as he had arrived.

"See you later, kids. I'll be back next week with some more fish," he said.

I hope not, I thought.

"Don't do us any favors," Carmella yelled as he backed the truck out of the driveway.

Sitting there in the yard, we were overwhelmed by a sense of despair as we contemplated the number of fish-head stew meals to come—a morbid thought that made us shudder.

With darkness now upon us, the crickets became noticeably louder, signaling it was time to head back into the house to retire for the evening. And, as we walked through the old screen door to the kitchen, our collective thoughts drifted toward the coming morning and what the new day would bring.

Charlene, Vincent, Kevin, Carmella, and Joanne

Chapter 3

The Grandchildren

*A*lthough our personalities were about as diverse as any could be, a strong sense of camaraderie still existed among the grandchildren. My sister Joanne was the eldest, and it was no secret she was Nana's favorite. Tall and attractive, she had long black hair, a slender figure, and a high energy level that was an asset when helping out around the house or watching the rest of us while Nana was at work.

A few of Joanne's responsibilities included feeding us, washing the dishes, and sweeping the floor. She was polite, always obedient, and did her best to maintain order whenever our grandmother was away from the house.

Jo was somewhat a homebody and her temperament was basically quiet, but, when she wanted something, she became excitable and overbearingly persistent. There were times when Joanne acted as if she were our second mother; not only did she demand to know what was going on, but she made it her business to find out what everyone was doing.

The Vineyard We Knew

Jo always used to complain about feeling cold; she was
sensitive to temperature and usually the first to notice any
chill in the air, particularly when we were by the seashore. No
matter how hot it was outside, to her, it was never hot enough.
The slightest breeze had Jo running to put more clothing on,
and, as sure as the sun rose in the sky each day, you'd see her
enshrouded by a coat—even while at the beach in her bathing
suit. My sister often sat in the sun for hours and baked away
without ever breaking a sweat. Because of her unique ability to
withstand what seemed to me intolerable doses of heat, I used
to jokingly call her the "Sun Goddess."

I really never knew if Joanne's physiology made her feel cold
all the time, or whether she was so self-conscious, she wanted to
be covered up. What I did know was that Jo's attire could make
you think the hot, humid days of summer were, in fact, the cool,
crisp days of autumn.

My older sister never hesitated to stand up for what she
believed, and she refused to let anything come between her and
what she felt she was entitled to. An example of this occurred
when our grandmother took her to a matinee movie one day.
Joanne, much taller than other kids her age, appeared to be
older than she actually was. The attendant in the ticket booth
at the theatre assumed she was over the age of twelve, and,
as required, charged the adult price for her ticket. Nana was
willing to pay for two adult tickets, but Joanne vehemently
protested because she knew she was entitled to the discounted
children's rate.

Joanne had the distinction of being the only one of the
grandchildren to have a legitimate, part-time summer job as a

teenager on the Vineyard. Joanne walked the three miles from
Oak Bluffs each afternoon to go to work as a dishwasher in
the sweaty kitchen of a restaurant called Stam's, next to the
Steamship Authority dock in Vineyard Haven. Her intention
was to get a job as a waitress at the restaurant, but that was
not an option for people of color; by design, it was reserved for
white kids only. Though dishwashing was not the most desirable
of menial jobs, it was one of a limited number of positions that
minorities could fill at the time, and it did provide my sister
with some spending change of her own.

✥

My brother, Chuck, was quiet and introspective as a boy. Tall
and thin with big bright eyes, he possessed an analytical mind
that was always in motion, always pondering, thinking. Chuck
had a reserved disposition, but he was driven—even at a young
age—to succeed at whatever he endeavored to do.

For some reason, Chuck's and Nana's personalities were as
incompatible as electricity and water; understandably then,
their relationship was not the most harmonious. Nana was
constantly on his case, and she disciplined him more often than
he deserved. Their tumultuous interactions provided me with
ample opportunities to exploit the situation, and I gladly took
any openings to reciprocate for misdeeds Chuck inflicted upon
me.

While at home during the school year, my brother and I
regularly had our skirmishes, and I was usually on the receiving
end of getting my butt kicked. But, during the summer months
on the Vineyard, revenge was mine. I knew that if I so much as

made a whimper, Nana would be on Chuck like white on rice—
ready to place blame—rightly or not.

There were times my grandmother seemed to have a grudge
against my brother, and she often treated him differently from
the rest of us. Could it have been related to the fact that he
resembled our father in appearance? That might have reminded
Nana of the struggles our mother had had to endure when our
father failed to live up to his paternal responsibilities. Or was
it that Chuck had an independent spirit Nana either could not
understand or refused to accept? It might have been just a simple case of bad chemistry between them. The true reason will
never be known, but, when it came to being reprimanded by our
grandmother, the only grandchild who had it worse than Chuck
was my cousin, Carmella.

On scorching hot summer afternoons, we were routinely
forbidden to go back into the house after being sent outside to
play, and, as a result, we grandkids had to find creative ways to
entertain ourselves as best we could. On this particular day, my
brother chose to play on the monkey bars in the schoolyard. He
climbed up, down, and across the tall iron structure. While on
top, Chuck playfully dangled his legs through the rungs as he
supported himself on the two rails under his arm pits. As he
engaged in his gymnastic pursuits, Charlene waltzed into the
schoolyard with Jo-Nancy, one of our island friends. Immediately recognizing an opportunity to have some fun, they turned
to each other and said, "Let's pull Chucky down."

They jumped up, grabbed his legs, and pulled him down
right on top of themselves. As the three of them tumbled to the
ground, my brother heard a loud "pop" in his shoulder blade.

Chuck, in great pain, slowly got to his feet and made his way back to the house.

"What happened?" my grandmother asked.

"I fell off the monkey bars and my shoulder hurts, Nana."

"Let me look at it." After checking his arm and shoulder, Nana said, "Don't be such a baby. I'll put some liniment on it and you'll be all right."

Our grandmother strongly believed in home remedies, and you had to be, almost literally, on death's doorstep to be taken to the hospital. Nana, as expected, dismissed Chuck's injury as being nothing more than a sprain. She sent him to bed, but not before smearing a tube of Ben-Gay all over his arm. That made the house smell like a hospital emergency room.

As the evening progressed, my brother's underarm swelled up like a balloon, and he endured excruciating pain during a sleepless night. It quickly became apparent that his condition was much worse than originally thought. Wincing with each attempt to move his arm or shoulder, he couldn't even make his bed the following morning.

As fate would have it, divine intervention brought my mother and stepfather unexpectedly down to the island the very next day. When Ma saw my brother, she asked, "What's wrong with you, Chuck-a-luck?"

To which he could only respond with a grimace.

My brother was immediately whisked off the island and back to Medford to get the medical attention he so desperately needed. When he was examined at the hospital, an x-ray revealed he had a hairline collarbone fracture.

There was, however, a silver lining to the story. Having been granted a furlough from "Carrie's Concentration Camp" because of his injuries, Chuck did not have to return to the island for the rest of that summer.

My cousin Charlene was a fun-loving young lady with an upbeat and pleasant demeanor, and her warm smile always projected a positive attitude. She had the kind of magnetism that made you want to be around her. Charlene loved Martha's Vineyard as a child, especially going to the Flying Horses, eating clams, buying candy at the penny-candy store, and hanging out with her long-time island friend, Becky.

Charlene's free spirit not only accentuated her individuality, but also encouraged her to dance to the melody of her own soundtrack. She had a dramatic side to her that was a positive attribute, particularly when telling a story or offering a descriptive explanation. She not only had the ability to communicate in a captivating manner, but her effervescence also provided many hours of levity that caused our stomachs to cramp up from laughter.

Charlene was shy as a young girl, and, because of Carmella's wheeling and dealing, she often found herself in situations she didn't understand, let alone know how to handle. When she was ten years old, she knew a boy in the neighborhood named Vinnie, who had a paper route that brought him by the house. Charlene thought he was cute, but wasn't old enough to express those kinds of feelings.

Carmella, fully aware of Charlene's immaturity, took it upon herself to play matchmaker by setting up an impromptu rendezvous at the house one afternoon when Nana wasn't home. While upstairs in the bedroom, Carmella handed Charlene a fancy cotton dress and said, "Charlene, put this on."

She complied.

Next, Carmella attached a pair of cheap, plastic earrings—a prize from a gumball dispenser—to Charlene's ears. Then she started applying lipstick to Charlene's lips.

"What are you doing?" Charlene asked.

"Just hold still, I'm almost done," she replied.

Minutes later, Carmella led Charlene downstairs to the living room, where Vinnie was sitting on the sofa, smiling from ear to ear.

"Hello, Vinnie," Carmella said.

"Hey, Carmella. Hello, Charlene."

"Hi, Vinnie," Charlene replied, not looking directly at him.

"Here, sit down next to Vinnie," Carmella told Charlene.

As they sat there, Charlene started to feel uncomfortable; at her age, she simply wasn't able to comprehend the situation. Not long after salutations were exchanged, Vinnie slowly placed his arm around Charlene, leaned over, and kissed her on the mouth.

"What are you doing?" she yelled as she pushed him away. Wanting no part of this awkward predicament, Charlene jumped up from the sofa and attempted to act silly, hoping to discourage any further advances from Vinnie. At that point, she no longer wanted him to think she liked him. Vinnie, with a sense of rejection, soon left the house.

Charlene turned to Carmella and asked, "Do you think Vinnie still likes me?"

After a brief pause, Carmella said, "He told me that he likes you even more now."

Charlene was horrified.

Nana was good friends with a lady a few houses away, and, on occasion, went over there to socialize. Often the two of them would partake in a cocktail or two while they gossiped about people and things happening on the island. One afternoon, after spending a couple of hours there, Nana came back to the house to prepare dinner. Chicken was on the menu that evening, and she went about the business of cleaning, seasoning, and tossing the chicken into a frying pan to cook it.

Charlene, noticing Nana's condition, quietly watched and soon realized she had overindulged in the consumption of alcoholic beverages. Our grandmother, in fact, was beyond the point of being tipsy—she was stone drunk. Nana kept a dirty red rag in the kitchen that she used to clean the floor, the counter, the stove, and anything else that needed to be wiped down. As she stumbled around the kitchen and grappled with the chicken, somehow that old soiled rag ended up in the frying pan.

"Nana, there's a rag in the pan with the chicken," Charlene said.

Nana looked at Charlene with disgust, and said, "That's not a rag. That's skin."

"Nana, that's not skin. That's the rag that you use to clean up."

"Don't tell me! That's skin—and you're going to eat it," Nana said, taking a swipe at Charlene.

That was the moment Charlene made it her business to inform the rest of us grandkids about what was going on.

We filed into the kitchen and took our usual seats at the

dinner table, but, as we did, Charlene looked at us with a distraught expression on her face.

"When Nana serves the food, don't eat the chicken," she whispered to us.

"Huh?"

"DON'T EAT THE CHICKEN; THERE'S A RAG IN IT!"

A few minutes later, Nana began serving the food as we watched her closely to see which of us would be the unlucky recipient of the filthy red rag.

After the food was served, Nana left the kitchen. Charlene, recognizing what was probably going to be her only opportunity, grabbed the rag-encrusted chicken from all our plates, threw it into a brown paper bag, and dropped the bag under the table, out of Nana's sight. Moments later, Nana returned to the kitchen. She had a curious expression on her face indicating she suspected something was awry, but her impaired cognitive ability prevented her from putting two and two together.

Charlene patiently waited for the right moment to snatch the bag from under the table and run down to the end of School Street as fast as she could. There she hurled the bag into the swamp, then made it back to the house before anyone knew she was gone.

Charlene's best Vineyard friend, Becky, lived a short distance from our grandmother's house. The two of them were always together—hanging around the neighborhood, going into town, or spending time at each other's houses—and sometimes Becky came along with us when we went to various places around the island, such as to the beach or to Gay Head.

A married couple in the neighborhood knew Becky's family.

When they were in need of a babysitter to watch their two young children one evening, they asked if Charlene and Becky would like to make some money, and, as expected, these two young ladies gleefully accepted and went over to their house to watch the kids. The parents, being somewhat liberal, didn't give a second thought to the abundance of alcoholic beverages they had at their house. And, as any normal teenagers would do, Charlene and Becky immediately took note of the impressive selection of libations neatly arranged in an oak cabinet with double glass doors.

After giving Charlene and Becky explicit instructions, the parents left the house for the evening, and the two inexperienced babysitters began watching the children, as agreed. When boredom from the summer television reruns became too much to bear, my cousin and her friend found themselves in search of a diversion.

"Charlene, do you feel like having a drink?" Becky asked.

"Sure. Why not?" Charlene said.

They took an inventory of the alcohol and settled on vodka, which they gulped down while the kids were upstairs asleep. Not long after, they started to feel dizzy and proceeded to climb the stairs to one of the bedrooms, where they passed out.

When the parents returned home later that evening, the sleeping babysitters were startled by being abruptly awakened. And now they had to make their ways home. Walking was very difficult because they were unaccustomed to the physical effects of alcohol. In addition to having blurred vision and spinning heads, Charlene and Becky felt nauseated and could barely maintain their balance.

Charlene's parents had arrived on the Vineyard that evening and were at the house when Charlene stumbled inside.

"Hi, Ma; hi, Dad," Charlene said, slurring her words.

"What's wrong with you? Are you sick?" her mother asked.

"I have to go to the bathroom," Charlene answered.

She wobbled into the tiny bathroom and quickly knelt down in front of the toilet. After vomiting into the toilet bowl, Charlene reached up and pulled the chain to flush the toilet. She then clutched her aching stomach with both arms and slowly crept up the stairs and fell into bed.

Meanwhile, over at Becky's house, the effects of her drinking binge played out in their own unique way. Unable to stand upright, Becky crawled through the front door on her hands and knees. Her brother Randy, after witnessing this spectacle, took the liberty of exposing her delinquent behavior to their parents. This resulted in a stern punishment for Becky, including confinement to the house for many days afterward.

✙

My cousin Vincent was a serious-minded, intelligent, and strongly opinionated boy, with a wiry physique, fair-skinned complexion, and light brown hair. Vince never hesitated to give you his candid opinion on any topic, and he could be brutally honest when doing so. Of all the grandchildren, Vincent was the only one who could push the envelope when it came to contesting Nana's authority. Whether through a subtle remark or the appearance of nonconformance, Vince knew just how far he could go before Nana would pounce upon him and extinguish any hint of dissonant behavior.

To Vincent, Martha's Vineyard was synonymous with two things: boats and the ocean. For him, they were the most important aspects about being on the Vineyard. His fondness for boats and making the trip from Woods Hole to the island were part and parcel of his Vineyard experience, as was being in or near the water that commanded the respect of all who dared to swim in its relentless currents.

Vincent had the ferry schedules committed to memory. He could look at a clock, and, regardless of the time it displayed, pinpoint the exact location of any of the boats traveling between Woods Hole, Martha's Vineyard, and Nantucket. One of his favorite things to do was hang out at the Steamship Authority wharf in Oak Bluffs and watch the arrivals and departures of the ferries.

At one time, the wharf was an enclosed wooden building that sat over the water; it was always dark, cold, and uninviting inside. The aesthetics of the wharf were forever changed when a huge fire roared through the structure and burned it down to the wooden pilings upon which it stood. When the new wharf was built, it was done with an open design, and the absence of walls and roof made it a much more pleasant place from which to catch the ferry.

When Vince was a teenager, he had a desire to work for the Steamship Authority and often visualized himself manipulating the ramp used by vehicles to drive on and off the ferries. My cousin knew every detail of the operations at the wharf, right down to the electric carts used to load and unload boxes of frozen seafood.

Vincent's curiosity, and his ability to analyze things that were

The New Bedford, Woods Hole, Martha's Vineyard & Nantucket Steamship Authority
Pier No. 9, Foot of School St., New Bedford, Mass.

SUMMER SCHEDULE

EFFECTIVE
JUNE 27, 1958 Thru SEPTEMBER 26

TELEPHONES
New Bedford .... WYman 6-8571
Woods Hole .... Falmouth Kimball 8-0710
Oak Bluffs .... Vineyard Haven 480
Vineyard Haven ..... Vineyard Haven 367

Paul W. Glennon, Chairman
C. Edward Hall, Falmouth   Robert M. Love, Martha's Vineyard
Robert E. Backus, Nantucket   Felix Perrone, New Bedford

Frank B. Lock, General Manager and Treasurer

While the Authority endeavors to furnish satisfactory service by keeping this schedule, times of arrival and departure shown herein cannot be and are not guaranteed. The Authority, therefore, is not responsible for failure to keep this schedule or for delays, inconvenience or damage resulting therefrom.

RESERVATIONS

Reservations for space for automobiles or for staterooms must be prepaid and may be made through the Authority's reservation bureau, Pier 9, New Bedford, or through the agents at the various stations. Reservations for automobiles may be cancelled if the automobiles are not at the pier one-half hour before scheduled sailing time at New Bedford and fifteen minutes before scheduled sailing time at other stations.

BAGGAGE

Personal effects to the value of one hundred dollars may be checked on each passenger ticket on payment of a small service charge. Through baggage may be checked to any point on this line to destination shown on passenger tickets except when the connection is with a bus.

FARES

Between	Adult One Way (tax incl.)	Adult 1-Day Round-Trip Excursion (tax incl.)	★Adult 2-3 Day Round-Trip Excursion (tax incl.)
New Bedford and Woods Hole	$3.80	$3.70	
New Bedford and Martha's Vineyard	3.55	4.30	$4.70
New Bedford and Nantucket	3.80	6.85	7.85
Woods Hole and Martha's Vineyard	2.20	3.15	3.65
Woods Hole and Nantucket	4.55	5.80	6.80
Martha's Vineyard and Nantucket	3.65	4.20	4.70

★Good Monday through Friday.

Half fare for children ages 5 to 11, inclusive.
All fares subject to change without notice.

TRAVEL GROUPS

Inquire about our special LOW COST Group Fares on application for 25 or more members of your club, school, or organization. CAMERA, BICYCLE or SIGHT-SEEING TOURS, BEACH PICNICS or OUTINGS. Contact our Ticket Agents, General Office or your Travel Agent for information.

FREIGHT AND PASSENGER AGENTS

NEW BEDFORD .... M. Shapiro
WOODS HOLE .... W. Simmons
OAK BLUFFS ....
VINEYARD HAVEN .... A. Huntington
NANTUCKET .... N. P. Giffin

AUTOMOBILE ROUTES

From New York to the Islands:

New England Thruoghway (Conn. Turnpike) to Providence. Via Taunton take Route 95 into 195 to 44 to 24 to Route 24. Continue on Route 28 to Falmouth and follow signs to Woods Hole.

From Boston to the Islands:

South on Southeast Express way to Route 128 North. Follow Route 128 North and turn off on Route 24 (Fall River Expressway), continuing to U.S. Routes 25 (Cape Cod) into State Route 28. Follow Route 28 to Falmouth.

Or follow Southeast Expressway into Route 3 and continue on Route 3 to traffic circle north of Sagamore bridge. Do not cross bridge but turn right and follow along the canal to first traffic circle. Turn right at Traffic Circle and cross Bourne Bridge. Follow Route 28 to Falmouth. At Falmouth, follow signs to Woods Hole.

CAPE COD

PASSENGER AND AUTO RATES

	PASSENGER FARES		AUTO RATES	
BETWEEN	Adult One Way	Adult 1-Day Round-Trip Excursion	One Way	1 Day§ Round Trip
WOODS HOLE AND MARTHA'S VINEYARD	$2.10	$3.00	$5.25	$13.00
WOODS HOLE AND NANTUCKET	4.30	5.50	8.50	22.50
MARTHA'S VINEYARD AND NANTUCKET	3.50	4.00	5.25	15.50

Half fare for children ages 5 to 11, inclusive.

All fares subject to change without notice.

§One day round trip automobile rates shown include 2 passengers.

TRAVEL GROUPS

Inquire about our special LOW COST group fares on application for 10 or more members of your club, school, or organization. Contact our Ticket Agents, General Office or your Travel Agent for information.

BAGGAGE

Personal effects to the value of one hundred dollars may be checked on each passenger ticket on payment of a small service charge. Baggage may be checked from any point on this line to local destination shown on passenger tickets.

WOODS HOLE, MARTHA'S VINEYARD & NANTUCKET STEAMSHIP AUTHORITY
P.O. Box 284 • Woods Hole, Mass. 02543

Winter Schedule

Effective Nov. 1, 1966 thru Jan. 3, 1967 All Times Local

FOR ADVANCE AUTO RESERVATIONS

From Mainland Phone
Woods Hole Terminal (617) 548-5011 ..... Boston (617) 426-1855
New Bedford (617) 996-8571 ..... New York (212) 966-1929

From Islands Phone
Vineyard Haven (617) 693-0367 ..... Oak Bluffs (617) 693-0125
Nantucket .... (617) 228-0262

STATEROOMS

Reservations for staterooms on the steamers may be made in advance through the reservation bureau at Woods Hole or may be purchased, if available, from the Purser on board the steamer.

LUNCH COUNTER SERVICE IS AVAILABLE ON ALL VESSELS.

FREIGHT AND PASSENGER AGENTS

WOODS HOLE .... J. Joseph
MARTHA'S VINEYARD .... N. DeBettencourt
NANTUCKET .... J. X. McHugh

highly technical in nature, occasionally placed him in potentially dangerous situations. As a result, his antics never failed to provide us with healthy doses of entertainment. One such incident occurred when Nana's stove was converted from oil to propane gas. Our grandmother could not get the hang of lighting the pilot, so Vincent kindly offered his assistance.

"Nana, let me help you. I can figure out how to light the pilot on the stove," he said.

"I don't understand. I can't seem to keep it lit; every time I try, the pilot goes out," Nana said.

"Nana, it's simple. All you have to do is open the oven door, hold a match over the pilot, and turn on the gas. I'll show you," he said.

After carefully assessing the situation, Vincent opened the oven door, and, to get a better view, wedged his head into a small compartment inside. While holding a lit match over the pilot, Vince turned the knob to release the gas. The fumes ignited in a flash, causing a ball of fire to blow back into his face. He instantly pulled his head out of the stove, his quick reflexes saving him from being seriously injured, but not before the flame burned his eyelashes off.

Vincent was three years older than I was, and sometimes I tagged along with him when he went into town. We'd visit the Steamship Authority wharf to watch the ferries arrive or go to the Oak Bluffs harbor to look at the boats moored there. We often walked along the boardwalk to compare the sizes of the boats and note any unique features and where they were from.

The Wesley Hotel, across the street from the harbor, had a

small donut shop out back where Vincent sometimes bought jelly donuts.

"Let's go over to the Wesley and get some donuts," he said.

Both surprised and excited, and acutely aware that my pockets were empty, I said, "Sure." It was good to know my cousin was kind enough to buy me a donut.

As we ran across the street, my mouth began to salivate at the thought of biting into one of the Wesley's huge jelly donuts, or perhaps a warm, soft, honey-dipped one, dripping with sugary glaze. After walking up a narrow road, we came upon a screened-in window at the back of the hotel. Looking though the window, I saw racks of donuts in every flavor imaginable, freshly cooked and oozing with sweet goodness. A lady lifted up the screen and asked, "Can I help you?"

"I'd like a half-dozen jelly donuts," Vincent answered.

The lady turned away, tore off a piece of waxed paper, picked six donuts from the rack, and placed them into a white paper bag. Vincent paid her and casually strolled over to me with the donuts in hand. He opened the bag, took out a donut, and began eating it. After consuming it in several bites, he reached into the bag for a second donut and gobbled it down, licking the granules of sugar off his sticky fingers as I stood there watching him.

It didn't take long before I got the sinking feeling he wasn't about to offer me a donut, as I had been led to believe. Not a single bite. Not even a hardened sugar-glazed chip that had fallen off the donuts and settled at the bottom of the bag. When the bag was folded closed and Vincent uttered the words, "Let's go," my hopes of tasting a donut that day came crashing down on me like a ton of bricks.

To make matters worse, Vincent had a habit of eating things that he enjoyed, such as desserts or sweet treats, very slowly—almost appearing purposely to tease as you watched him savor each bite in a manner that suggested the willful act of conspicuous consumption—all while he commented about how *good* something tasted.

~

Cousin Carmella was a young girl who was many years beyond her chronological age. She had an average build and wore her dark brown hair pulled back into a big braid. To say Carmella had an outgoing personality was an understatement. She was the rebel of the bunch. Her mission in life was to defy any semblance of order or discipline, and it was she who presented our grandmother with the greatest challenge. Carmella was the architect of most of the fireworks at the house on any given day, and she won first prize when it came to the number of whippings received—and there were many.

The product of a broken home, Carmella had been taken in and cared for by my Aunt Florence and Uncle John after her mother passed away. Carmella didn't have a shy bone in her body, and she often conducted herself in ways that would raise the eyebrows of even the most uninhibited person. For example, she thought nothing of being seen with no clothes on. There was a game she used to like to play, "Explore the Body," in which she would casually lie down on a bed and expose herself to inquisitive onlookers for a detailed study of her physical anatomy—an intimate show-and-tell of her most private of bodily parts.

The Grandchildren

Carmella's hormones must have been kicked into overdrive early on because her interest in older boys was quite apparent. While most girls her age were content with tea parties, dollhouses, and Easy-Bake ovens, our cousin would have none of that. This frisky young lady was obsessed with trying to sneak boys into the house at night or when Nana was at work.

Carmella often slept in the same bed as Charlene. One night they had gone to bed just as on any other night. However, Charlene later woke up because she had to use the bathroom. When she turned over to get out of bed, she was shocked to see a strange boy lying there between her and Carmella. Speechless at first, Charlene just looked at the two of them and finally said, "Hello."

She crawled over them, jumped out of the bed, and went downstairs, where she fell asleep on the sofa until the next morning.

On another hot summer's night after the lights were out and we were all in bed, I was awakened by strange sounds coming from the bedroom at the front of the house where Carmella, Joanne, and Charlene slept. A heated discussion was taking place, and, beneath the whispers, I heard the rattling sound of a ladder being hoisted against the front of the house.

"Carmella, you know you shouldn't be bringing boys into the house. You're going to wake Nana up and get us all in trouble!" Joanne whispered.

"Don't tell me what to do, Joanne. Shut up and mind your own business!" Carmella said, in a vindictive tone.

"Carmella, are you in there?" A voice was heard coming from outside.

It was Willie from next door, whose desire to get a little "nooky" had made him take his chances by climbing up the ladder to the bedroom window.

"Shhh . . . don't talk so loud. My grandmother will hear you!" Carmella said.

"Okay, okay. Can I come in now?" he asked.

"Yes, but be quiet!" Carmella whispered back.

Before Willie could get even one foot through the window, our grandmother ran into their bedroom at lightning speed, a baseball bat in her hand, and yelled, "You get the hell out of here!"

When she got to the window where Willie was poised to sneak in, Nana swung the bat like a major leaguer and knocked him upside his head, causing him to roll off the porch and fall to the ground with a thud. Looking down at him, wrenched in pain from the blow, our grandmother said, "Don't ever come to this house again!"

Willie sprang to his feet and, cradling his injured left arm, hobbled away as fast as he could.

Nana then turned her attention to Carmella, and we all knew what was coming next.

"Who do you think you are, trying to sneak boys into the house?" Nana asked.

"But, Nana—"

"I'll teach you to try a stunt like that again," Nana snapped.

Carmella's eyes began to well up as our grandmother grabbed her by the arm and dragged her downstairs to the kitchen. All the way from upstairs, we heard that old, familiar whipping sound of the strap being used to administer punishing blows to Carmella, who was screaming, "No! No! Nana, please!"

The Grandchildren

After inflicting several lashes upon Carmella, our grand-mother said, "Now get upstairs and go to bed!"

Carmella—still reeling from the sting of the strap—ran up the stairs, jumped into bed, and cried herself to sleep.

〜

My sister Deirdre was a bright young girl with pretty cocoa brown skin and a strong will. Determined, she did things her own way and didn't care much about what others thought, even when she was young. Dee's memories of the Vineyard are some-what different from those of the rest of the grandkids because her time on the island occurred when my other sister, brother, and cousins had reached an age at which they no longer spent summers with our grandmother.

Dee made her first appearance on the island when she was one month old. My mother and stepfather came to the Vineyard on an August afternoon with her all bundled up in a blanket and introduced her to the family. It was the first time any of us had seen her.

For some reason, when I learned her name was Deirdre, I had a difficult time pronouncing it. It is also worth noting that, upon her arrival, I was officially no longer referred to as being the "baby" of the family—a designation gladly relinquished by me and passed down to her.

It wasn't until Dee was several years older that she spent a couple of summers on the Vineyard with Nana. Prior to that, her visits to Oak Bluffs were made with my mother and stepfa-ther and were usually short in duration.

Some would argue that Dee was fortunate not to have been

subjected to the same living conditions and strict discipline the rest of us endured for so many summers. Still, her brief time there marked her indelibly nevertheless. You might say she experienced the waning years of the wrath of our grandmother, comparable to being on the outer edge of a hurricane, where the effect, while not very potent in terms of intensity, still leaves a lasting impression. For example, in what might have been a flashback to the days when Nana took care of the rest of us, she made Dee neatly fold her facecloth and towel after washing up each morning.

Deirdre's relationship with our grandmother was cordial, and the responsibility of having to care for a slew of grandchildren was not a factor for Nana when Dee stayed with her. With the absence of the chaos that existed when the rest of us were there, it was a much quieter time, and Dee and Nana were able to do many things together, such as play Chinese checkers or Crazy Eights, engage in an afternoon of berry picking, or simply hang out and eat jelly donuts. Dee was even amused each time Nana poked a pinhole in the shell of an egg and sucked the raw yoke and egg white out.

To Deirdre, it wouldn't have been morning at Nana's house if she didn't smell fresh fish, lightly breaded with flour and cornmeal, being deep-fried in hot oil, or hear grits bubbling on the stove, along with the sound of Nana whisking eggs that would soon become the main ingredient of a hearty breakfast. On some mornings, Nana sent her down to Whiting's Dairy to buy a carton of milk for her cereal; on such trips, Dee ever-so-cautiously avoided going past the end of School Street for fear of receiving a stern reprimand.

The Grandchildren

Deirdre and Corey

If there was one thing Dee *never* looked forward to when she stayed with Nana, it was having her hair combed. Its coarse texture—although a better grade than the kinks I had on top of my head—still required some coaxing to get it to do what my mother or grandmother wanted. I can recall Dee spending many hours sitting in a chair back home while Ma pulled a hot comb through her hair. Screams of discomfort and the nauseating smell of burning hair filled the room as my mother attempted to make Dee's hair more manageable. The fact that she was on the Vineyard did not save my sister from the ritual, and now it was Nana who had the pleasure of accomplishing the task. She would bop Dee on the head with the comb every time she attempted to escape the painful raking action of Nana's strong hands.

Not surprisingly, my sister and I had our share of sibling squabbles at Nana's house. We would argue and tattle on each other in a perpetual tug-of-war to get one another into trouble. I was usually the one who got reprimanded because I was older, and, as such, should have known better.

For many years, I felt Deirdre was overly protected by my mother and stepfather, but, in time, I found that not to be true. Instead, I realized it had simply been a case of "older brother" syndrome, in which I felt I was to blame for any arguments that occurred between us.

>~~

When I was young, my personality resembled a coin; it was two-sided, with distinctly different characteristics on each side. I was by no means a schizophrenic, but traces of duality were inherent in me.

One side of my personality was that of an introvert; I had an incredible imagination and was quiet and shy. Most of the time, I minded my own business and just went with the flow. The other side, however, clearly contained the more aggressive, outgoing traits of a wiseass punk with a temper that, if provoked, could explode in an instant and rise like solar flares from the sun.

Being the sixth grandchild in a pecking order of seven, I was an easy target for taunting or teasing by my older siblings and cousins. Any disagreements I had with them—and my resulting anger or hurt feelings—were usually deserved because of my stubbornness.

There weren't many weapons at my disposal to retaliate when my siblings and cousins ganged up on me, but, one evening, after engaging in an argument that left me upset, I threatened to run away. Nana was at work and it was just us kids at the house.

"I'm going to run away and you all will get in trouble when Nana finds out," I said.

"Go ahead. Nobody really cares if you run away or not," Joanne replied.

Feeling like a victim and with tears in my eyes, I left the house and ran across the street to hide in the bushes. There I sat for several hours, hidden from view in the thicket, but able to see the house and yard perfectly. As the day went from dusk to dark, the kitchen door swung open and out they came, frantically engaged in a spontaneous search party.

They took turns calling, "Kevin! Kevin, where are you?"

"We'd better find him before Nana gets home," Joanne said.

They fanned out from the yard in different directions, desperately calling out to me, but I was having a ball just sitting tight and enjoying the show.

"Nana's going to kill us!" Charlene said.

"It wasn't my fault Kevin ran away," Vincent said.

"It doesn't matter whose fault it was; we're all going to get a beating if we don't find him by the time Nana gets home," Chuck said.

"Kevin, where the hell are you?" Carmella yelled.

After about an hour of searching, and as the last tinges of light faded away, they returned to the house, having failed to find me, to ponder their fate.

"I can't believe he really ran away. I didn't think he had the nerve," Joanne said.

"Me neither. We didn't tease him *that* much," Chuck said.

"I always thought he was kind of nutty, anyway," Vincent said.

"Don't talk about my little brother like that," Joanne said.

"Sorry," Vincent replied.

As the blame game continued and their concern for my whereabouts reached a fever pitch, I sat quietly in the bushes—until I saw car lights come down Pacific Avenue and turn into the driveway. The moment for which I had been patiently waiting had arrived; my grandmother was finally home. She walked into the house with a slow gait, and I could only imagine how they were trying to explain what had happened to me.

In a rare moment of empathy, I emerged from the bushes and ran across the street to the house, where I was greeted with open arms by my brother, sister, and cousins, relieved I had not run away or that nothing adverse had happened to me. But, deep down inside, I knew their gratitude was rooted in the fact that they were not going to be punished as they would have

been if I had actually run away, or, worse, something untoward had happened.

In terms of my own relationship with my grandmother, I was neither her most nor least favorite grandchild; I fell somewhere in the middle. I received no preferential treatment from Nana, for I can recall numerous instances of being slapped or beaten

Nana and me

with the strap in support of her unwavering belief: if you spare the rod, you spoil the child. As kids, we didn't have to worry about being spoiled because the rod was *never* spared. That adage was taken to great heights by our grandmother, who hardly ever shied away from the opportunity to discipline her grandchildren.

Our Grandmother

Chapter 4

Carrie White

*O*ur grandmother's name was Caroline, but her friends called her Carrie. She was a stern and independent woman with an old-school mentality and little tolerance for disrespect or foolishness. Born in Boston, Massachusetts, in 1895, Nana had a strong temperament, and there was no mistaking how she felt about things. Carrie had no problem expressing her rigid, nonnegotiable opinions to anyone who had the nerve to engage her.

I can remember how she bolstered her position on a topic by ending her statements with the interrogative, "Am I right or wrong?" If you were stupid enough to answer that question in any way but the affirmative, then it wouldn't be long before you wished you had answered appropriately. She was not the type to let things be easily forgotten, and was quite adept at reminding you of any differences of opinion that might have irritated her long after an incident had occurred.

Carrie's physical attributes were not uncommon. She was a healthy, plump little woman with olive skin and straight black and gray hair. She wore colorful cotton dresses and didn't hesitate to put on a sweater, no matter how warm it was outside. Her flimsy eyeglasses were held together by pieces of Scotch tape wrapped around the frames, and the lenses were marred by scratches and imperfections from many years of use. She had strong hands for an older woman, an attribute she had developed while working as a welder at a naval shipyard in Boston during World War II.

Nana's first trip to Martha's Vineyard occurred in 1935. She was forty years of age at the time and went there to visit her friend Isabel, Carmella's mother. Isabel owned the house at 48 Pacific Avenue in Oak Bluffs, but, some years later, Nana acquired it by taking over the mortgage due to Isabel's inability to keep up with the payments. Every year thereafter, Nana spent summers on the Vineyard and winters with my aunt, uncle, and cousins in Boston.

During the winter months, Nana anxiously waited for spring to arrive so she could make the trip to the island to enjoy her solitude, tend to her garden, entertain friends, and host the family over the course of the summer. There was always something going on at 48 Pacific Avenue; that summer house saw more than its share of activity every year, especially when my brother, sisters, cousins, and I were there.

Our grandmother loved playing cards and board games, and she spent countless hours doing so. Although she never hesitated to take part in card games such as whist and gin rummy, solitaire was one of her favorites because she could play it by herself. Carrie was also an avid fan of Chinese checkers and dominoes, games she patiently taught us all how to play. The challenge of keeping six grandchildren occupied on inclement days was made a little easier by these inexpensive, tried-and-true forms of entertainment. I can vividly recall spending many hours playing these games at the kitchen table and on the front porch.

Nana was a creative individual, and she made colorful bowls and place mats out of glossy pages she cut out of old magazines. This was a labor of love. She tore out pages from popular magazines of the day, such as *Look* and *Life*, and cut them into narrow strips. These she rolled into small, round tubes which she shellacked. After the tubes dried, she meticulously tied them together with string, crafting them into various configurations resembling stars, rectangles, and ovals. Nana generously gave away her artistic creations to family and friends, and it wasn't unusual to see her handiwork on display at any number of residences on the Vineyard or back home in Boston.

Every evening after dinner, our grandmother fed scraps of food to seagulls that happened to be in the vicinity. She offered them fish, chicken, or beef bones, as well as skin, vegetables, moldy bread, spoilage from the refrigerator, and just about anything else we did not eat. The scraps were usually piled onto a plate, brought out to the backyard, and dropped on the ground. Seagulls were efficient at consuming the remnants—like flying eating machines—and we looked forward to observing their competitiveness each time they were fed.

There was a telephone pole at the beginning of the driveway where a lone seagull would perch to see if a meal would be offered. But, as soon as the kitchen door swung open, flocks of these gray and white scavengers appeared from out of nowhere. Although literally hundreds of seagulls flew over the house on any given day, Nana would say that she was going to feed "Gooney," the pet name she gave to a particular seagull that, according to her, arrived each evening to be fed. She believed Gooney to be the same bird that came to the house day after day, but, as far as we were concerned, Gooney could have been any one of a thousand birds. That was an argument we dared not engage her in. Instead, we refrained from going down that path by simply keeping quiet.

Nana's bedroom was the only room in the house with wallpaper, a colorful medley of blue, pink, and beige print. (All the other rooms had bare wooden walls full of knots, characteristic of the lumber used to construct them.) A simple double bed, supported by a metal headboard and footboard, stood against one wall. Next to it was a nightstand, upon which an alarm clock and a table lamp sat. A dresser with a mirror was positioned along the opposite wall, and on top of the dresser was a small jewelry box.

Nana rose each day at five thirty sharp. She put on her bathrobe, made her bed, and quietly eased down to the kitchen from the second floor. Her morning routine included manually lighting the oil burners on the stove and putting on a fresh pot of coffee. She would then open the kitchen door and go out to the yard carrying the dirty dishwater from the previous day. She poured it on her flowers, and this homemade liquid fertilizer seemed to work well because all her plants thrived—they were healthy, vigorously blooming, and bursting with color.

Upon returning to the kitchen, Carrie checked the mousetraps under the cabinet to see if any of the little critters had been caught during the night. Next, she brushed any rodent droppings off the countertop and swept them up from the floor before scrubbing down the entire kitchen. Prior to making breakfast, Nana always turned on the radio to listen to the local news, weather, and tide report.

Ding, ding . . . ding, ding . . . It's now 6:00 a.m. on Radio 1030. Today's weather will feature sunny skies, highs in the mid- to upper eighties; very humid with a slight chance of a passing shower or thunderstorm on the Cape and islands; high tide will be at 1:00 p.m.

There were times Nana took me into town with her after breakfast to go to the post office, stop at the bakery, and pick up a few groceries at the Reliable Market.

"I'm heading into town and Kevin is coming with me," Nana would say to my siblings and cousins. "Make sure you all make your beds, wash the dishes, and sweep the kitchen floor before you go out to play. And stay near the house," she ordered. "We'll be back in a couple of hours."

"Yes, Nana," they would answer.

Nana and I left the house to begin our trip into town. We walked slowly across the sandy schoolyard to the top of School Street, a small wire-mesh shopping cart in tow. The translucent morning fog hovered close to the ground, creating an illusion of disorientation and weightlessness. As we strolled through the mist, I felt the heaviness of the humid air pressing down on my lungs each time I took a breath.

School Street was on a hill that was level at the bottom but became quite steep near the top. As a result, going into town was always easier than the return trip, when the climb back up the street took its toll on many a traveler, especially on hot summer days.

This particular street was unique because it had a sidewalk with a curbstone on both sides. Most of the streets in Oak Bluffs—excluding those in downtown—did not have sidewalks; they were usually bordered simply by sandy shoulders that lay on either side of the road.

About a quarter of the way down School Street was a dirt road called Second Avenue. Here some of the neighbors' houses were located, including the summer residence owned by the grandparents of my longtime childhood friend Jackie Byard, who, ironically, lived just two doors down from my house back in West Medford.

After walking past Second Avenue, my grandmother and I continued to the end of the street where tall stands of cattails and elephant grass grew ten- to twelve-feet high in a swamp. Whiting's Dairy, a local business selling fresh eggs, milk, and butter from local farms, was at the corner on the right-hand side of the street.

Diagonally from Whiting's Dairy, on the opposite corner, was a laundry that resembled an army barracks. White curtains, hanging loosely from rods that stretched across the tops of the open windows, gently flapped back and forth as the wind flowed through. We could hear a low, humming sound coming from the washing machines and the sewing machines in use on the first floor of the building, and the loquacious workers inside also disrupted the morning calm as they washed, pressed, and stitched clothing.

A young woman, apparently taking a break, sat on an old wooden chair being used to prop open one of the doors. Her fair skin was flushed by the intense heat inside, and she displayed an expression of relief as a cool breeze gently caressed her face.

Around the corner from the laundry we entered the site of the Martha's Vineyard Camp Meeting Association, also known as the Campground. Established back in the 1830s by a Methodist religious organization as a place where members could pitch tents, in time it replaced the crude, flimsy tents with small, colorful gingerbread cottages built so close together, they looked as if they were attached to each other. The Tabernacle—a towering, open-air structure in which church services, community sings, and performances were held throughout the warm summer months—stood in the center of the Campground, surrounded by the quaint gingerbread cottages.

The grounds were made up of neatly manicured lawns, exotic gardens, sprawling oak trees, and beautiful flowers. A narrow circular road surrounded the Tabernacle; it resembled a huge cul-de-sac, on which railroad tracks that once carried trolley cars through the Campground were exposed by cracks in the pavement.

After exiting the Campground, we followed a short walking path to an underpass that cut through a building called the Arcade. At the other end of the underpass was Circuit Avenue, the main street in downtown Oak Bluffs. Stores, restaurants, and shops lined both sides of the street, and it was always congested with cars and pedestrians.

Our first stop was always the post office, where my grandmother picked up her mail from a small combination box in the hallway, just around the corner from the general delivery window. The air inside the post office was musty, and it wasn't unusual to run into people you knew. This day was no exception.

"Carrie? Carrie!" a voice shouted. It was Lillian, one of my grandmother's friends.

"Good morning, Lillian. What brings you out so early?" Nana asked.

"I've got a busy day ahead. I need to take care of some important business before noon," she responded. "But, listen, I'm taking a drive up-island this afternoon. Would you care to come along for the ride?"

"I wouldn't mind going, but my grandchildren are at the house. And, besides, I'm working this evening; perhaps I can go with you another time."

"Okay, I'll stop by the house this afternoon before you go to work," Lillian said.

"I'll see you then," Nana replied.

My grandmother carefully dialed in her alphanumeric combination, opened the door to the mailbox, took out the correspondence inside, and firmly closed the door.

"We need to go to the bakery now," Nana said, as we walked out the door of the post office.

"What are we getting at the bakery, Nana?" I asked.

"Jelly donuts," she responded.

Jelly donuts were my grandmother's favorite kind, and she managed to scrape together some spare change to buy them every now and then.

The Corner Store was a few doors down from the bakery. In the display window was a red, battery-operated motorboat I always stopped to admire, each time hoping it would still be there. Today, just as I had done so many times before, I stared at the boat through the window, almost in a trancelike state. With the burning desire of a child, I envisioned myself carrying it to the beach and floating it on the water while other kids watched me with envy. Without warning, I was jolted out of my daydream by my grandmother's hand pulling me along.

"Come on, Kevin, let's get to the market," she said.

As I was being yanked away from the window, the realization that there was no money for such things created a void deep within me. My only recourse was to look at that boat through the window whenever I had the chance and imagine what it would be like to float it in the calm waters of Nantucket Sound.

Our last stop was the Reliable Market, a local family-owned grocery store Nana patronized on a regular basis. Their prices were reasonable, given that most things on the island were twice as expensive as they would be if purchased on the mainland. Nana was friendly with the owner's wife, Helen, who always worked the cash register at the checkout line. She was a soft-spoken, petite woman who wore eyeglasses and always had a rubber thimble on her index and middle fingers to help her count money. Helen was kind enough to occasionally let you "pay her next time" if you happened to be a little short on cash for what you needed to buy. This honor system created goodwill between the store and local residents and went a long way to preserving the viability of both the business and customers alike.

Nana picked up the items she needed and wheeled the shopping cart to the checkout line where Helen was waiting to ring up her goods.

"Good morning, Carrie," greeted Helen.

"Hello, Helen. How are you today?" asked Nana.

"I'm just fine, thank you. Did you find everything you were looking for?"

"Yes, thank you."

"Hello, Kevin. My goodness, you're getting *so* tall."

"Hello," I said.

Nana kept her money in a worn leather pouch wrapped in a tightly knotted handkerchief. Whenever she wanted some cash, she took out the handkerchief, carefully untied and unfolded it, and got what she needed from the pouch. After paying for the groceries, we placed them in the cart and left the store to begin our walk back home.

It was just before noon, and the sun was almost directly overhead. Passing through the Campground again, we briefly stopped to sit under the cool shade of the Tabernacle. It was always peaceful there, and the slightest sound reverberated throughout the entire structure. Because of that, I used to like to clap my hands or yell out loud to hear the effect. After quietly sitting there for a while, Nana said, "We'd better be on our way."

After leaving the tranquility of the Campground, we turned three corners and approached the bottom of School Street. As we looked up at the long, steep climb that awaited us, the intensity of the heat rose from the blacktop, looking like transparent waves as the sun radiated up the entire length of the treeless street. Once we began that laborious walk up the hill, there was no stopping or turning back. Long before reaching the top, I would feel my sweaty feet slipping and sliding as they burned within the suffocating confines of my rubber-soled sneakers. It was as if we had walked over red-hot coals as we painfully traversed the long, uphill slope. Finally, with home clearly in sight, we picked up the pace and walked across the schoolyard and into the house.

As we entered through the kitchen door, an eerie quiet greeted us; this was a sure sign no one was home, and, once again, I found myself in search of something to do.

"Nana, can I go outside?" I asked.

"Yes, but don't go too far," she replied.

My first thought was to track down my brother, Chuck, or cousin Vincent. As a kid, I always wanted to hang out with them, but, because they were older, they were not always amenable to having me tag along. There were times, however, they were forced to tolerate my presence.

I left the house to begin my search, and, almost immediately, I felt the afternoon heat descend upon me, turning my energetic bounce into a slow stroll. While passing by the cesspool in the backyard, I smelled a pungent odor seeping through a crack in the steel cover, and I did my best to avoid breathing in the funk by blocking my nose with my fingers.

Continuing on, I attempted to guess where my brother and cousin might be. One of the places I was usually sure to find them was at the school next door, where they often congregated with friends at the bottom of a stairwell. The temperature in the shade down there was usually ten to fifteen degrees cooler than above ground, and it provided cover from the hot sun that could easily turn your skin to a deep, dark brown in a matter of minutes. As I approached the stairwell, the usual banter of young voices I expected to hear was conspicuously absent. When I peered down the stairs, the only visible activity was a small rabbit that startled me as it quickly hopped away.

Disappointed by my failure to locate them, I decided to cross Pacific Avenue and head over to the cemetery. There I climbed up onto a stone pillar at the entrance. Thick branches of mature maple trees hung over the spot where I was sitting, and countless seedpods showered down upon me as the wind blew them off the trees, causing them to fall in a rapid, spinning motion, like miniature helicopters. The small space under the canopy of leaves was cool, and I was adequately shielded from the sun.

As I sat there, I looked both ways down the street for any sign of life, but it was just too hot outside, not unusual during summer days on the Vineyard. Turning my attention to the cemetery in back of me, I noticed an old cannon sitting on the grass next to a pile of black cannonballs neatly stacked into the shape of a pyramid. A white flagpole, a gold eagle on top of it, rose from the ground and displayed a tattered American flag that gently flapped in the slow, hot wind. A green pipe fence surrounded the cemetery on all sides except in back, where the edge of the forest formed a natural wooded barrier. Treelined paths, embedded with multicolored stones, separated the sections of burial plots in the cemetery. Old headstones and crypts of various sizes were symmetrically positioned throughout, and I heard the sound of a lone lawn mower sputtering as it cut the grass nearby.

In all likelihood, the man pushing that lawn mower was John Barboza, a quiet, older gentleman who lived across the street from us with his wife, Mary, who was twenty-two years younger than he was. As caretaker of the cemetery, Mr. Barboza was responsible for burying the caskets of the deceased after they were lowered into the ground—a task we used to assist him with, on occasion. He also kept the grass trimmed and ensured that the grounds were neat and clean. Mr. Barboza was quite competent at what he did; he was always at the cemetery early in the morning, going about his work of trimming, cutting, watering, cleaning up, and repairing broken sprinkler heads or anything else that needed attention.

I used to walk through the cemetery to read the names and dates on the headstones, which offered me a glimpse of people who had transitioned from this life. The dates spanned hundreds of years, revealing the brevity of some people's lives and the longevity of others. It often made me wonder about the circumstances surrounding each person. Who were they? What did they do in life? Who were they related to? How did they die? A litany of unanswerable questions filled the recesses of my mind, leading only to more questions.

Just the thought of being alone in a cemetery might easily conjure up morbid impressions of ghosts and goblins, particularly at night, but I was quite comfortable being there. Perhaps it was living right across the street that made me immune to it, or maybe the "bucket brigade" runs to get water at night had strengthened my fright tolerance. We grandkids often rode our bikes through the cemetery in the dark of night—to the unindoctrinated, potentially a scary proposition. For me, that old cemetery was a peaceful refuge where I found comfort in my own solitude; it was a place of quiet contradiction, where I often thought not about death, but about life, its purpose, and how I fit in.

After having spent a couple of hours in the cemetery, I made my way back across the street and headed for the house. All I could think about was getting a glass of water to hydrate my parched throat. When I got there, I opened the screen door and went into the kitchen, where I found my grandmother and her friend Lillian, whom we had met at the post office earlier that morning. They were sitting at the table gossiping about Lillian's latest pursuits and conquests.

Lillian, who lived up the street next to the cemetery, was an extrovert with a flamboyant personality. She smoked cigarettes incessantly, had a nagging cough, and came across as being somewhat disingenuous. Lillian was known for her flirtatious ways, and it was no surprise that she had several "gentlemen acquaintances" among whom she effectively distributed her time. Nana's friend dabbled in real estate and always seemed to have some scheme in the works. As usual, my grandmother's conversation with Lillian came to a screeching halt once I was inside.

"Hi, Nana. Hello, Lillian," I said.

"Hello, Kevin. How are you today?" Lillian asked.

"Fine, thank you," I answered. "Nana, can I have some water?"

"Yes, you may." Nana went over to the sink with a plastic cup and held it under the faucet to fill it with water. She handed it to me, and I grasped the cup with both hands and raised it to my lips. The cool water soothed my throat as it slid down, then extinguished the intense fire in my gut.

"Carrie, I'm out of cigarettes. I'll have to run to the store to get some more," Lillian said.

"Don't worry about it; Kevin will go to the store for you," Nana replied.

I will?

"Kevin, you don't mind running down to S. S. Pierce for me, do you?" Lillian asked.

What was I supposed to say? That I wouldn't go?

"Sure, I'll go. I don't mind," I said.

"Good. Here's twenty-eight cents for a pack of cigarettes. Remember to ask the clerk for Lucky Strikes. When you get back, I'll give you a little something for going," she said.

Reluctantly, I began walking to the store in the blazing heat. It was so oppressive outside, even the leaves on the trees appeared to cower for some relief from the sun as a steady, hot wind blew over the landscape. The thought of getting a nickel, or perhaps even a dime, for my efforts buoyed me as I slowly trudged through the schoolyard and crossed School Street. After following a path through the field, I came upon a sandy road that led to Washington Park. From there, I saw the store at the bottom of the hill on New York Avenue and made my way down the grassy slope.

I bought the cigarettes and immediately retraced my steps back to the house. The walk was torturous. I started to feel faint as I climbed the hill, sweating profusely from the heat that felt as if it were radiating from a blast furnace. My breathing was labored, and I became light-headed as I inhaled and exhaled in concert with each step. At that point, I contemplated falling to my knees and crawling the rest of the way up the hill, but something within me made me press on.

The cheerful sounds of chuckling and laughter greeted me at

the door when I got to the house, but, as expected, Nana and Lillian abruptly ended their conversation when I entered.

"You're back already? That was fast!" Lillian said.

"Here are your cigarettes," I said.

"Thank you, sugar," she replied.

Lillian snatched the cigarettes from my hand and immediately pulled on the cellophane strip to open the package.

"Kevin, why don't you go back outside and play?" Nana said.

At any other time, I would have jumped at Nana's directive, but I hesitated because I wanted to get paid for going to the store. While making my way to the door, I timidly looked back to see if Lillian caught my slow response as a cue for her to make good on her promise. All she made good on was sticking a cigarette between her lips, lighting it with a match, and deeply inhaling the noxious tar and nicotine. That mechanical act was followed by her blowing a huge puff of smoke into the air.

Feeling deflated and taken advantage of, I left the house.

What a bitch, I thought.

Looking beyond the front of the house, I noticed an area of shade under an apple tree and slowly walked over to sit down and escape the sun's deadly rays. There I found relief while waiting for the long, hot summer day to pass.

As it turned out, I never got paid for running that errand, and, after that, whenever Lillian was around, I made damn sure I wasn't.

Chapter 5

The Leather Strap

*H*anging loosely from an old rusty nail on the wall in the kitchen was an inanimate object that had a staunch effect on our behavior as kids. Perhaps never before had something so unassuming created the amount of terror this object did. The leather strap, as it was called, was a simple garrison belt that found its way into our young lives through the good intentions of my brother, Chuck. And as the saying goes, "The road to hell is paved with good intentions."

So it was in this case.

That thin strip of rawhide saw more action over the course of a decade than anyone—including us—could have imagined. At one time destined to lay lost in a thicket off a sandy road next to my grandmother's house, this belt was inadvertently discovered by my brother, who decided to pick it up and bring it into the house to give to Nana. This gesture of goodwill would surely earn him high marks and place him in the most favorable light in Nana's eyes, thereby rewarding him with a break from her strict, disciplinary ways.

Not in a million years.

That fateful day—when Chuck presented Nana with his unique gift—was the day an ordinary belt became known as "the strap." This metamorphosis occurred the moment Nana took ownership and customized it to her liking by using a pair of scissors to make two separate lengthwise cuts in the last third of the belt. The resulting three dangling strips of leather were very effective at inflicting stinging blows that produced red welts, similar to those that appeared after a horsewhipping.

Some of us grandkids got our butts tenderized by the strap more often than others, but none of us were completely immune to it. The whippings we received gave new meaning to the terms "rump roast" and "chuck steak," for the flesh on our bones could have rivaled either of those cuts of beef with respect to being tender.

The strap spent just as much time off the wall as it did on, and there was a litany of reasons Nana used it, including not eating, talking back, being flip or disrespectful, not doing what you were told, arguing or fighting among ourselves, feeding unwanted food to the dog, not being back home on time or when called, and touching things you weren't supposed to, or, even worse, breaking them.

Although the strap hung silently on the wall, its mere presence psychologically screamed at us—providing instruction about what to do or what not to do—in effect, molding and shaping who we were, how we acted, and who we ultimately became.

One delightful summer afternoon, Nana baked a delicious deep-dish blueberry pie with a buttery, golden brown crust to die for. In fact, Carmella almost did.

This pie was made with fresh island blueberries that grew deep in the woods—blueberries we had collected during one of our berry-picking expeditions. Nothing compared to the taste of a homemade pie packed with plump, juicy berries bursting with flavor.

After dinner, Nana gave us each a small slice of the pie, mindful that there were six of us grandkids. This required her to meticulously cut and distribute the pie to ensure we all received an equal amount. What's more, this rationing made certain that there would be enough left for another serving. Before leaving for work that afternoon, Nana cleaned up the kitchen, wrapped up the pie, and put it away. A short time later, her ride picked her up, and we kids were left to hang around the house and entertain ourselves as best we could.

Apparently, Carmella still had that "blueberry pie kind of feeling," a temptation that proved to be too great for her to resist. She went back into the house, took out the pie, and carefully cut a thin slice no bigger than a sliver. Carmella picked up the slice with her fingers, gently placed it in her mouth, then licked the remnants of blueberries from her lips.

"Don't tell Nana I took any of the pie," she said, as the rest of us watched in amazement.

"All right, but, if she asks any questions, you're on your own," Chuck said.

"Not to worry; the slice I took was so small, Nana will never know," Carmella said with confidence.

"For your sake and ours, too, I hope you're right, Vincent said.

Later that night, Nana arrived back home. Fully aware of Carmella's earlier mischievous activity, we kids became anxious as Nana paced around the kitchen. Quietly listening from the bedrooms upstairs, we heard Nana getting settled after a hard day at work, taking off her sweater and apron, hanging them on a hook on the wall. Next came the familiar squeaking sound of the refrigerator door opening, then closing.

"Who took some of this pie?" Nana asked.

No one uttered a word.

"You kids get down here right now!"

Immediately obeying our grandmother, we ran downstairs to the kitchen to confront her allegation.

"I'm going to ask you all one more time. Who took some of this pie?" We glanced at each other with dumbfounded looks on our faces, but no one said a thing—until Vincent decided to question the validity of Nana's accusation.

"Nana, how do you know if any of the pie was taken or not?" he asked.

"Don't even *try* to mess with me, boy; I know exactly how much was left, and somebody took some," she said.

Our grandmother had to have measured the pie with a ruler before she left for work because the slice Carmella had taken was so thin, there was no way in the world you could tell any of it was missing by simply looking at it. In fact, Nana reacted as if the whole pie had been eaten. In an instant, she was standing in front of the strap on the wall, saying, "If I don't get a straight answer from someone, I'm going to beat each one of you."

She reached over, removed the strap from the nail, and

slowly wrapped one end of it around her right hand. My heart started racing as I envisioned her whacking away at our hides, beating us into oblivion. At that moment, something came over Carmella, because she acted completely out of character by admitting that she had taken the pie. Consequently, the rest of us were spared from receiving a serious ass-whooping.

As expected, Nana went to town on Carmella and spanked her as if she had stolen more than just a piece of pie. And while Carmella was being horsewhipped, I could almost feel the sting of the strap as the loud snap from each vicious stroke shot right through me, making me cringe as Nana waled away on her amidst the screaming and crying. As I said, that golden-crust pie was to die for . . . almost.

We have all been in circumstances that made us do things we might not otherwise have done. My brother, Chuck, often found himself in these situations through no fault of his own. Most of the time, it was because of the incompatible chemistry that existed between Nana and him; they simply didn't get along.

Chuck's life on the island mimicked that of a poor young soul stuck on a constantly rotating merry-go-round that stopped only three times a day—at breakfast, lunch, and dinnertime—in order to allow bouts of culinary torture to be inflicted upon him. Eating Nana's meals was always an ordeal for him because odds were, seven times out of ten, Chuck despised what was being served, and, ten times out of ten, Nana forced him to eat every bite.

As a result, my brother was the last one to leave the dinner table because of his reluctance to consume any number of our grandmother's signature dishes. Whether it was hominy grits, rice cereal, fish cakes and beans, kidney beans and rice, Hungarian goulash, or fish-head stew, to him, it was all the same— inedible slop.

Late one afternoon, the rest of us, having long ago finished our meals, were in the backyard with a few friends from the neighborhood. Chuck was still inside at the table. He had watched us eat; now he was squirming in his chair as he and Nana engaged in their usual—for him, still *pre-meal*—face-off. This was the recurring theme played out at the table more often than not, causing my brother a level of anxiety that, by today's standards, would be called child abuse.

"Chucky, eat your food. You're not moving from that table until you finish everything on your plate," she said.

With a sad expression on his face, Chuck looked down at his plate and began playing with the food. He stirred it, mashed it, and created designs in it with his knife and fork as he tried to think of a way to get out of eating it. The dog was outside in the yard, so that was out. Desperately wanting to get outside with the rest of us, Chuck was well aware of the fact that that was not going to happen until he ate the food. He forced the last mouthful down his throat, then, without saying a word, looked over at Nana with daggers in his eyes and held up his empty plate to show her he had finished his meal.

"Good. You can go outside now," she said.

Chuck got up from the table and ran outside to join the rest of us. Still quite upset, he didn't seem to care who might hear him as he expressed his disgust.

"I *hate* her," he said as he came out of the house.

It soon became clear that one of our so-called friends in the yard was no friend at all.

"Ooh . . . Nana White . . . Chucky said that he hated you," she said.

At that point, Nana immediately appeared in the doorway and asked, "What was that you said?"

"Chucky said he hated you," she repeated.

"Shut up. I didn't say that," Chuck nervously replied.

Nana barged out of the house, grabbed Chuck by his arm, and dragged him back inside.

"So, you hate me, huh?" she asked.

"I didn't say that, Nana."

As if by magic, Nana instantly had the strap in her hand, cocked and ready to go. She had an amazing command over that strap, almost as if she could will it off the wall and into her hand without ever having to reach for it, similar to Darth Vader's ability to make things move by using his mind, as depicted in the *Star Wars* movies.

With a captive audience outside in the yard, and Nana's unwavering commitment to exercising her disciplinary privilege, she showed us all who was the boss as she lashed away at my brother for engaging in behavior she considered to be blatantly disrespectful.

I often wondered if Nana actually believed, through some warped sense of logic, that beating Chuck would somehow change his feelings toward her, or that her merciless whacks would transform his seething anger into some kind of love or admiration. The only thing it succeeded in doing was pushing them farther apart, widening the divide between them with each painful stroke of the strap.

><

My siblings, cousins, and I were subjected to a strict set of rules that our grandmother enforced with an iron fist, and there wasn't a day that went by when one of us didn't get reprimanded for something. If you were smart, you would lie low for as long as possible, trying to stay below Nana's radar.

One evening, I made an unwise decision that violated Carrie's Rule #68, which required you to get your ass back in the house when the streetlights came on. That particular rule, although firmly ingrained in my subconscious, somehow became irrelevant as I allowed myself to be mesmerized by the shiny new headlight I had just installed on my bike.

Having failed to notice that the sunlight had faded away and dusk had fallen upon our sleepy little neighborhood, I continued pedaling—up and down the streets, over paths and through the fields—completely enamored by the narrow beam of light that lit the way as I cycled over familiar terrain. Unfazed by the distinct sound of crickets chirping all around me, I kept my evening bike ride going strong until the shrill voice of my grandmother echoed across the schoolyard and pierced the depths of my soul.

"Kevin! Kevin!" Nana called, repeatedly.

I raced to the house in a panic, terrorized by the thought of being punished for not getting home on time. Barreling down the driveway, I noticed a dim light filtering through the screen door. Nana was sitting at the kitchen table, peering out the small window when I arrived.

"Kevin, where have you been?" she asked.

"I was riding around the neighborhood," I said.

"Didn't you hear me calling you?"

"Yes."

"Why were you not home on time?"

I said nothing.

"You know you should have your butt at home when the street-lights come on. I shouldn't have to be looking for you."

"I know, Nana."

What I *didn't* know was that Nana had the strap hidden under the table in her lap. In the time it took me to blink my eyes once, I heard that familiar whipping sound of the strap being swung against my arms and legs, followed by a painful stinging sensation that felt as if I had been attacked by a swarm of bees. I spun around, ducked, and danced in an attempt to avoid being struck, but I found no relief from the blows or escape from my punishment.

"I'm sorry for coming home late," I whimpered, as tears flowed down my cheeks.

"Now, when I tell you to be home when the streetlights come on, that's what I mean. Am I right or wrong?" she asked.

"You're right, Nana," I replied.

After shaking off the painful effects of the strap, I limped up to my room to contemplate how my stupidity had gotten me in trouble again. What I learned from that experience was to pay attention to details, like the setting sun or when the streetlights come on. Or the chirping of crickets, telling me the day is done.

Chapter 6

The Marables

*S*eventy-five yards to the south of my grandmother's cottage was a weathered ranch house that had survived more than its share of harsh winters. The steps leading to the porch were missing, and the task of entering or exiting the house had to be accomplished by either stepping up two feet to the porch, or scaling several milk crates haphazardly positioned as makeshift stairs.

Attached to the side of the house was a dented oil tank that provided fuel for heat and cooking. A rusty bicycle frame—one wheel missing—was positioned upside down on the ground as if someone had been working on it but neglected to finish the job. Discarded tire rims were strewn across the yard, adding to the milieu of clutter characteristic of the property.

This was the home of the Marables, a family of nine who were year-round residents of the island, all inhabiting this tattered old house together. They could best be described as being the "black" version of the Beverly Hillbillies—without the oil fields, mansion, swimming pools, cars, or movie stars. An adaptable bunch, they were more than capable of living off the land, for they cultivated a large vegetable garden.

Mr. Marable worked odd jobs around town, and Mrs. Marable took care of the household. They did their best to support their family and were resourceful when it came to meeting the challenges that life on the Vineyard put before them.

There were five brothers in the Marable family—Ansin, Hubie, Roy, Benji, and Willie—and two sisters, Fauna and Jasmine. They were typical kids, each with their own unique personalities and talents, but all of them also seemed to have an edge to their personas, making them come across as rough, outdoor types.

Ansin had a reserved disposition and was the most intellectual of the bunch. He voraciously read volumes of books and magazines, and knew practically every answer to questions about history, math, science, geography, and current events; this young man was the incarnation of a walking encyclopedia.

Ansin used to stroll down to the Flying Horses almost every day, and he always carried a portable radio/tape recorder on his shoulder that repeatedly played a song called, "The Happy Piano." This particular musical composition consisted of an upbeat, irritating melody performed on a single instrument—a pipe organ—with no accompanying instrumentation. Listening to a few measures of that song had even the staunchest music lovers running for cover to escape the monotonous drone characteristic of the tune. The problem I had wasn't that he enjoyed the song; what annoyed me was the fact that it was the *only* song he ever played. When I asked him why he always played the same song over and over, his answer was simple—he said he liked it.

When Ansin arrived at the Flying Horses, he turned off the tape recorder and placed it on the floor next to a trivia game he loved to play. From that moment, he was all business. Ansin not only played that game, he owned it. After comfortably positioning himself in front of the machine—tightly wedged between rows of pinball machines—he reached into his right pocket, pulled out a single quarter, and inserted it into the coin slot to begin playing. Trivia questions popped up on the screen, one after another, covering a wide range of topics, each having to be answered in a matter of seconds. Incredibly, Ansin knew all the answers and usually responded long before the allotted time had expired.

He stood in front of that machine for hours at a time and won so many replays, it would have taken him days to play them all, if it were even possible to do so. His knowledge base was so extensive, this bright young man rarely, if ever, gave an incorrect answer. Crowds gathered around and watched in amazement as he made the machine look inept by answering each question flawlessly. Ansin's command of the subject matter often made the game hesitate as it struggled to compile another question in a futile attempt to stump him. When he grew tired or bored after playing for several hours, he simply stepped away from the trivia game, grabbed his tape recorder from the floor, flipped the switch, and resumed listening to the same song for the umpteenth time.

After Ansin made his way out the door and down the stairs

of the Flying Horses, any games he had won were left for anyone who wanted to take a shot at playing them. On one occasion, I attempted to play a game he had left, foolishly thinking
I could somehow replicate his brilliant performance. Silly me. I
quickly learned that my IQ was no match; I was outwitted in a
matter of minutes.

><

Fauna, the older sister, was the consummate tomboy. She always
competed with her brothers, and, regardless of whether it was
chopping wood or climbing trees, they had nothing on her.

In fact, many times I witnessed her getting the best of them
when they engaged in one of their favorite pastimes, wrestling
matches. Somehow, she always prevailed by wrapping her arms
around their necks and placing them into suffocating head-
locks, forcing them to give up. This was one girl you didn't
mess with.

Fauna was strong for a female, and, although her voice had
a tone that could cut right through you, her personality was
outgoing and pleasant.

><

Jasmine was the youngest child in the family, and, unlike her
older siblings, she was quiet and shy. She often played in the
yard, or by the side of the road that was made of sand and
crushed clamshells.

Her little round face, chestnut brown skin, and short curly
hair resembled the features of a doll, but were often obscured
by the clouds of dust that floated through the air and settled

on her petite body every time a car or one of the tractor-trailers from Rogers Trucking passed by.

Willie and Benji were the two oldest brothers in the family, and they kept a regimented schedule; we didn't see them very often because they were usually working.

Each day, these two young men left the house early in the morning and did not return until well after dark. They were responsible for helping to support the family, and, with their strong physiques, did jobs that involved manual labor, such as landscaping, making deliveries, or working down at the docks.

Unassuming types, they easily blended in with the rest of their family and pretty much did their own thing.

Roy and Hubie were the youngest of the brothers and closest to my age. More often than not, they were involved in some sort of mischief. They each had bully tendencies and looked for any excuse to start a fight or engage in heckling us for no particular reason. Whenever we saw either of them coming down the road, we could bet that trouble wasn't far behind.

I never quite understood why they were so hostile to us. Perhaps they resented our invading *their* turf every summer, or maybe it was because they didn't know us well enough yet. But that was all about to change.

Hardly a day went by that we didn't find ourselves ducking from a barrage of rocks that the Marable clan hurled into our yard—sometimes hitting their mark, sometimes not. My brother,

Chuck, got hit in the head with a rock thrown by them when he was only four years old. After years of having to tolerate these unprovoked attacks—and being a little older ourselves—we decided to retaliate against our aggressors. Initially, we threw rocks back at them, to no avail. Then, after reconsidering how to deal with them, we recruited four of our summertime friends to assist us.

One afternoon, we crouched down and hid in the tall elephant grass adjacent to Nana's house and waited for our adversaries to meander by. Before long, Roy and Hubie approached the place we were hiding, and, when they got close enough, we jumped out of the grass and ambushed them. While pinning them down, we proceeded to beat the living crap out of them, until, after several minutes of exchanging punches and rolling around on the ground, they broke away and ran home.

We congratulated each other for finally standing up to these bullies, but our victory celebration was short-lived, because, almost immediately, we saw Mrs. Marable briskly walking toward Nana's house with her two sons in tow. She called out to our grandmother long before reaching the house; she was determined to convince Nana to reprimand us for what we had done.

Nana, however, was steadfast in her defense of us because she had known all along that Mrs. Marable's sons were responsible for perpetuating the years of discord that existed between the two clans. After a lengthy discussion about the merits of what was and was not acceptable behavior, a truce was agreed to, and, as of that day, we became good friends with our rough-and-tumble neighbors.

Gay Head Cliffs

Chapter 7

Gay Head

*I*t wasn't unusual for any of my grandmother's friends to stop by the house unannounced; that's how it was on the Vineyard—kind of staid and neighborly. This was particularly true on days when Nana didn't have to go to work and she could devote her attention to relaxing or socializing.

One of her good friends was Walter Norris, a stout and jolly old soul with dark brown skin, a gruff voice, and a thick salt-and-pepper mustache. More often than not, he'd have a fat stogie sticking out of his mouth, and the unmistakable aroma of cigar smoke never failed to alert us to his presence. Mr. Norris was actually Nana's boyfriend, but she would *never* admit to such a thing. To us, he was simply . . . Nana's friend.

Ranger Norris, as he sometimes referred to himself, always showed up at the house in a black '59 Chevy and took us to places that could only be reached easily by car. It might be the beach one day or a spontaneous drive around the island the next. Countless times he took us to the airport, but not to board a flight or even to watch planes take off and land. The only reason we went there was to buy eggs.

On the far side of the airport were several rows of long, single-story buildings lined up next to one another. When we got out of the car and went inside, it felt as if we had entered an overcrowded tenement house for chickens, in which hundreds of clucking hens laid fresh eggs for customers to handpick and take home. Many of the breakfasts Nana prepared for us began with a trip to the airport—compliments of "Ranger Norris."

Mr. Norris's arrival at Nana's house was always a production. He would aggressively maneuver his vehicle into the driveway by making a sharp left turn off Pacific Avenue, then honk the horn a couple of times. As the car rolled toward the house, it kicked up a big cloud of dust before coming to a stop. This routine reminded me of a scene from a Western, in which a group of cowboys would ride into town on galloping horses that stopped in front of the local saloon amid clouds of dust, while, in the background, you'd hear the subtle sound of an old, out-of-tune player piano softly tinkling away.

After Mr. Norris arrived at the house, he opened the car door and stepped out, sporting a pair of worn blue jeans, cowboy boots, and what he called a ranger's hat—the kind Smokey the Bear wore.

"Helloooo there! Is anybody home?" he shouted, as he opened the screen door to the kitchen.

"Hi, Mr. Norris," greeted my sister, Joanne.

"Hello there, young lady. Is your grandmother in?"

"Yes, she's on the front porch. I'll go tell her you're here."

Amused by the presence of this larger-than-life character

who resembled a giant teddy bear, we just kept staring because we didn't quite know what to make of him. While waiting for Nana to make her way to the kitchen, Mr. Norris struck up a conversation. "Hey kids, have you ever heard of the Ranger's Trail?"

We glanced at each other and shrugged our shoulders in a manner that indicated we had no idea what he was talking about.

"Well, there's a dirt road down yonder that snakes through the woods, and the rangers use it to ride horseback while they're on patrol. One day I'm gonna take you all down the trail with me to check it out. It'll be fun!"

"Hello, Walter. How are you today?" Nana asked as she entered the kitchen.

"Afternoon, Carrie. I'm about as fine as fine can be. You all feel like going up to Gay Head?" he asked.

We were hoping she would accept his invitation.

"A drive up-island would be nice. You kids go put your bathing suits on while I make some sandwiches to take with us," Nana said.

We dashed upstairs as fast as we could, slipped on our suits, and grabbed our towels, goggles, flippers, floats, and anything else we could carry to Mr. Norris's car. Before leaving, Nana prepared an assortment of sandwiches—tuna, peanut butter and jelly, bologna, egg salad—which she packed into a picnic basket to be taken along for the outing.

Moments later, we kids crammed into the back seat of the car and jockeyed for position, indiscriminately climbing over one another and knocking each other out of the way in an attempt to secure one of the preferred seats next to the windows. Inside the car, we noticed a spider dangling in the middle of a silky web. Mr. Norris, taking note of our curiosity, discouraged us from disturbing it.

"Don't kill that spider," he said.

"Why not?" Vincent asked.

"Because it's my friend," Mr. Norris answered.

"Aren't spiders dangerous?" Charlene asked.

"They can be, but this one isn't. He rides around with me and keeps me company," he replied.

After that bizarre verbal exchange, Mr. Norris started the car and we were on our way.

The twenty-two-mile drive to Gay Head took us down winding country roads, over rolling hills, and through lush green forests as we traversed the towns of West Tisbury and Chilmark. A pine-scented breeze circulated through the open car windows as the powerful eight-cylinder engine purred down the back roads like a tamed lion. None of us were bothered by the fact that we were wedged so tightly together; we could easily have been mistaken for interlocking pieces of a jigsaw puzzle. Looking out the window, we saw beautiful stone walls extending gently over the terrain, with post-and-beam fences delineating the numerous farms that sprang up along the way.

The sun played a game of peekaboo as it filtered through the leaves on trees that stood straight up as we zipped past them. We spotted grapevines growing along the side of the road for miles, and picturesque inlets, carved out by the pristine ocean. We barreled up the road that led to the Gay Head Cliffs, where the old brick lighthouse—with its rotating red and white beacon—stood high on a hill above the ocean. This was the definitive sign that we had finally reached our destination. Just beyond the lighthouse, Mr. Norris pulled the car over to the side of the road and parked.

The Gay Head Cliffs were on a peninsula at the southwestern tip of Martha's Vineyard. Whenever islanders talked about going there from any of the so-called "down-island" towns of Oak Bluffs, Edgartown, or Vineyard Haven, they referred to the area as being up-island, regardless of the fact that, strictly speaking, one had to travel southwest to get there—not to the north, as logic would dictate.

The original year-round residents of Gay Head were forebears of the Wampanoag Indians, and the cultural and economic attributes of these early Native Americans were evident in the current residents' specialized boating and hunting skills, as well as the handmade clothing, jewelry, and bottles of red clay they sold at the cliffs.

Because of their stunning beauty, the Gay Head Cliffs—formed by a glacier that extended over North America thousands of years ago—continue to be a natural wonder and a popular tourist attraction for island visitors. The face of the cliffs is composed of sand, gravel, and clays of various colors, and was once part of the ocean floor. The receding motion of the glacier forced the sediment upward and created the cliffs as they stand today. Only a fraction of their original height due to erosion and human activity, the Gay Head Cliffs are now protected by federal law that prohibits climbing them or removing clay.

However, when we were young, there were no such restrictions to prevent us from climbing up, down, or across the magnificent cliffs. We often scaled the fossil-encrusted rocks and slid down the slippery slopes—free to play to our heart's content and immerse our bodies in the moist, red clay.

"It's time to hit the beach. Everybody out of the car!" barked Mr. Norris.

We opened the doors and sprang out like clowns popping out of a jack-in-the box. Making our way down a long, winding path toward the shore, we eventually came upon our favorite spot, a section of beach that provided easy access to the cliffs towering above us and the cool relief of the invigorating ocean below.

As soon as the blankets were spread on the sand, the fun began. For hours, we swam, built sandcastles, took clay mud baths, ate sandwiches, collected seashells, skipped rocks, buried each other in the sand up to our necks, and chased and threw each other into the water, nearly drowning ourselves in the pounding surf.

"Okay, troops, let's hit the cliffs!" Mr. Norris yelled out.

That was his not so subtle way of challenging us to climb the steep cliffs all the way to the top where the lighthouse stood. Initially, my brother, Chuck, balked at the idea. The rest of us—not knowing any better—began the perilous climb to the top like sheep being led to slaughter.

"I can't climb up these cliffs," Chuck uttered with a trembling voice.

"Sure you can," Mr. Norris said, with a hearty laugh.

"Come on, Chuck! Let's go!" we all prodded.

"You can do it; it's easy," Vincent said.

I don't know if it was the positive reinforcement or just blind faith, but Chuck finally agreed to make the upward climb with the rest of us. We started out by carefully grabbing on to the boulders with our hands and placing our feet into any crevice we could find, being wary not to slip on the wet, slimy clay. One such error could have hurled us back to the bottom like snow tumbling down a mountainside during an avalanche.

The higher we climbed, the steeper the slope became. The only way to make it successfully to the top was to keep climbing and not look down—for any reason. We heeded that advice and eventually reached the top of the cliff where the lighthouse stood on an open field of fertile grass.

The view overlooking the ocean from this vantage point was awe inspiring. A tiny island, known as Noman's Land, appeared in the distance opposite a small chain called the Elizabeth Islands. Massive round boulders, easily weighing more than a ton each, were deposited along the seashore by glacial movements during the Ice Age. Some of the boulders jutted out of the water like the heads of prairie dogs peeking from their burrows, and the clay on the cliffs displayed vivid hues of red, orange, gold, gray, and brown, giving them a dazzling effect as the sunlight reflected off them. The vibrant palette of colors blended together as the always-moist clay "melted" and slowly oozed down the face of the cliffs and into the sea.

The climb back down to the beach was pure exhilaration for us kids. With the force of gravity tugging at us and the moist clay serving as a natural slide, we slipped and slid down the paths all the way to the bottom in a matter of minutes, all of us completely smeared from head to toe in the colorful gook. After reaching the beach, we jumped into the ocean and rinsed the clay off our bodies.

With the sun drifting lower in the western sky, we dried ourselves off, packed up our belongings, and hiked back to the car for the return trip home. It was almost dark by the time Mr. Norris dropped us off, and some of us—totally exhausted from the day's activities—had to be abruptly awakened after having drifted off to sleep during the ride back. The car entered the driveway and slowly came to a stop in front of the house.

"You all thank Mr. Norris for taking you to Gay Head today," Nana said.

"THANK YOU, MR. NORRIS," we recited, amongst the yawns, stretches and sleepy eyes.

"You all are welcome—any time!" he replied, with a big smile. "I'll see you again soon."

We got out of the car and lazily made our way to the house, but, before going inside, I turned around and watched Mr. Norris as he backed out of the driveway. A high-pitched, whining sound emanated from the car as it moved in reverse, and a large plume of cigar smoke mesmerized me as it floated up from the driver's side window and disappeared into the cool evening air.

Mr. Norris drove down Pacific Avenue and quickly disappeared from sight. As I walked toward the house, I thought about how he truly was our link to the rest of the island. His willingness to shuttle us around allowed us to experience the Vineyard in a way that we otherwise would never have known. Ranger Norris facilitated our intimate knowledge of Martha's Vineyard, and for that we were eternally grateful.

Chapter 8

Land of Fruit and Berries

*M*other Nature provides sustenance for all living things, and my siblings, cousins, and I were perfect examples of that.

Whenever hunger pangs caused our empty stomachs to growl, the wonderful bounty of fruit that grew on the island was not only an attractive alternative to some of the meals we were forced to eat at Nana's, but it was plentiful and easily within reach.

Vast orchards of crisp apples and pears dotted the land-scape, and miles of grapevines—bursting with big, juicy, red and green grapes—grew all over the island. The tartness of a Granny Smith apple on your tongue, or the rejuvenating taste of a sweet Bartlett pear, was as easy to attain as climbing up a tree. The tantalizing fragrances emitted by the ripened fruit tickled our olfactory nerves and made us feel as though we were experiencing nirvana.

Countless open fields in which various fruit-bearing trees grew, were within walking distance from the house. There were no roads one could follow to get to these fields—only narrow, sandy paths etched over time by thousands of footsteps left by those traveling back and forth over the same routes.

Once there, we literally spent hours climbing trees and picking the fruit right from their limbs, consuming as much as we desired while sitting on thick branches and dangling our feet with not a care in the world. There was no need to worry about ingesting pesticides because they weren't used here. Our biggest concern was the potential of finding a worm lurking deep within the fleshy part of the fruit. And we were careful not to disturb the swarms of honeybees as they buzzed about, collecting pollen from the blossoms, because we did not want to get stung.

Whenever we ventured into the woods only a short distance from the house, we also found basketfuls of succulent blueberries, blackberries, and strawberries just waiting to be picked and turned into delicious homemade pies and jams.

The abundance of undeveloped land in Oak Bluffs allowed us to lay claim to the fruit that grew there; it was ours for the taking. We encountered objections from no one, and it wasn't unusual for us not to see anyone walking through these fields for hours.

These orchards not only allowed us access to the fruit, but also provided us with a place to let our imaginations run free. It was the perfect setting for childhood games such as hide-and-seek, cowboys and Indians, or army. They also served as a quiet retreat in which to duck temporarily out of sight until we heard Nana's voice through the trees as she summoned us to return home. The only price we had to pay for all this was the time spent picking the fruit—and the wrath of Nana when we weren't able to eat our meals because our appetites had been spoiled by Mother Nature's sweet nectar.

After spending several hours gorging ourselves on apples and pears one afternoon, we were sitting on the ground, leaning back against trees, enjoying the soothing sounds of nature, contented as a herd of cows in a pasture. As we basked in the warmth of the summer sun—blue skies and creamy white clouds above us—the melodic sound of our grandmother's voice echoed through the trees and snapped us to attention.

"Nana's calling us; we'd better get home," I said.

We ran back to the house as fast as we could and found Nana standing on the front porch.

"Come in and eat. Supper is ready," she said.

Reluctantly, we trudged into the kitchen, took our places around the table, and waited for the food to be placed before us.

"I cooked some Hungarian goulash for supper tonight," she said.

"That's just great," Chuck whispered under his breath.

"What did you say?" asked Nana.

"I didn't say anything, Nana," he replied.

Hungarian goulash was a fancy term our grandmother used to describe "leftovers." It was actually remnants of food from previous meals combined to make a stew. Each time Nana prepared it, you could bet it contained something different, depending upon what we had eaten during the past week. Needless to say, we were not happy campers.

"I can't eat this food; I'm too full from eating all those apples," Carmella whispered.

"I can't either," Vincent whispered back.

As a stalling tactic, I tried to identify every ingredient in my bowl.

"Hmm . . . let's see what we have here: corn, carrots, noodles, peas, celery, onions, peppers, kidney beans, lima beans, rice, chunks of beef, broth—"

"Stop playing around and eat your food, Kevin," Nana said.

"Nana, I have a stomachache," I said.

"You'll have a behind-ache to go along with your stomach-ache if you don't eat," she said.

Taking her response as a warning, fully aware I was otherwise facing the sting of the strap, I forced the first spoonful of goulash down my throat. Then the second. And the third. My stomach began to twist and turn, and, once again, I felt as if I were going to throw up. I wasn't the only one at the table having difficulty eating. My brother, sister, and cousins were all showing signs of distress at the prospect of having to force down the food, prompting Nana to ask, "What's going on here? Why aren't you all eating?"

We offered no response other than blank stares.

"Don't tell me you were eating those apples again. I've told you time and time again about doing that; those green apples will make you sick. Now, if this *ever* happens again, I'm going to whoop the whole bunch of you until you straighten up and fly right!" she said.

In a rare empathetic gesture, she excused us from the table and allowed us to go back outside. As we gleefully skipped out of the house thinking we had gotten over Nana, she said, "I'll put this food away for your supper tomorrow."

Oh, no; not that, I thought.

Land of Fruit and Berries

It didn't matter what type of scheme we kids were able to conjure up—Nana always had a way of making us obey and play by *her* rules, either through verbal directives or the ever-persuasive sting of the leather strap. The fact that we were actually subjected to this kind of discipline might be met with a tinge of skepticism, but, as Nana used to say, "If I'm lying, I'm flying!"

Enough said.

Chapter 9

Little Boy in Drag

One of the most difficult challenges for me to overcome as a boy occurred on the Vineyard when I was about nine years old. The challenge in question wasn't the type in which you learned how to do something through repetition and practice, such as taking your first steps, tying shoelaces, or riding a bicycle. This was one that required me to *unlearn* something I had developed as a bad habit that not only affected me, but also other members of my family. My grandmother wasn't about to tolerate this foolishness, and she made it a priority to address the problem.

Getting me to stop wetting the bed—an inexcusable form of behavior—required drastic measures. That I engaged in this activity was surprising, since I was old enough to know better. But, at that time, three elements were wreaking havoc on me as they battled for supremacy in my subconscious mind—fear of the dark, fear of getting a beating, and plain laziness.

Sometimes it really was laziness that kept me from dragging myself out of bed at night to go downstairs to the bathroom when nature called. But, as a child, I had a vivid imagination, and so, most often, it was my fear of the dark that prevailed over the fear of being punished. Lying there in bed, I would be awakened by the urge to go to the bathroom, but the pitch-blackness that surrounded me paralyzed my limbs, making it nearly impossible for me to move. This fear was so pervasive, I strained to hold my water until the mounting pressure in my bladder made me feel as if I were about to explode.

Some nights, drifting in and out of slumber, I would awaken to a warm, wet trickle flowing down my leg. This would slowly seep through my pajama bottoms, saturating them until they became soggy and cold. Now the sheets and mattress were also a soiled, yellow-stained mess.

Each time this happened, I received a painful beating from Nana. The sting of the leather strap felt like a whip as she forcefully swung it against my tender young skin. After several spankings and the realization that this form of discipline was not producing the intended result, Nana decided to take a different approach to rid me of this bad habit, once and for all.

"You wet the bed again?" Nana snapped, a look of disbelief on her face.

"Yes," I responded, as I lowered my head and looked toward the floor.

My body became rigid in anticipation of being struck again, but I was surprised when Nana didn't reach for the strap as she had done so many times before. In my naïve attempt at rationalization, I thought she might finally be mellowing with age, or perhaps she felt an uncharacteristic sense of empathy for me.

This time, instead of whacking me with the strap, Nana began lecturing me. "Kevin, you're too old to be wetting the bed. There's no excuse for it; you should be ashamed of yourself! I'm boiling some bathwater, so go upstairs and take off those dirty pajamas."

Obeying her command, I climbed the stairs and made my way to the bedroom. Feeling totally worthless, I just stood there and looked at the soiled sheets still on the bed.

I heard Nana making several trips between the kitchen and the bathroom as she filled the tub with hot water that had been boiled in a huge pot on the stove. After she carefully balanced the proportions of hot and cold water, she reached a tolerable water temperature—one just right for me to take a bath.

I walked down to the bathroom, stepped into the tub, and slowly eased myself into the steaming bathwater. I reached over and grabbed one of the old, worn-out facecloths from the towel rack on the wall and began washing the urine off my body.

"I'll be right back. I'm going to get some clothes for you to put on," Nana said.

She returned ten minutes later with articles of clothing that clearly didn't belong to me and placed them on the sink.

"Nana, those aren't my clothes," I said.

"I know they're not, but you're wearing them today," she replied.

I jumped out of the tub, and as I stood there dripping wet, Nana began drying me off with a towel. Then, after helping me slip on my underwear, Nana reached over and picked up my new outfit—a powder blue cotton dress with lace trim.

As the gravity of the situation became apparent to me, I yelled, "Nana, that's a dress! Boys don't wear dresses. Girls wear dresses!"

"Girls and *sissies* wear dresses, and, since you wet the bed, you're a sissy. Now stand still," she said, as she smacked me on the butt.

Nana lifted the blue dress up over my head and pulled it down onto my small frame. Instinctively, something told me this wasn't right, and, as I witnessed myself being dressed up like a little girl, I started to cry. My river of tears, however, did not affect my grandmother in the least, and, after she led me to the kitchen, she placed a pink bow on top of my head, securing it with several pieces of Scotch tape.

Being forced to wear a dress in the house was shocking enough, but, when Nana opened the screen door to the kitchen to make me go outside, I was petrified. Still, faced with only two options—go outside and be completely humiliated, or stay in the house and get beaten within an inch of my life—I chose the former.

After being ushered to the door by my grandmother, I reluctantly left the safety of the doorway and stood frozen with my back tightly pressed against the side of the house. In a panic, I glanced around to see if any of my friends were in the vicinity as I desperately searched for a place to hide; there was no way I wanted to be seen wearing this pretty dress and fancy bow. As fate would have it, I immediately heard a high-pitched voice echo across the schoolyard.

"Kevin, is that you?"

There was no need to see who was asking the question because I knew the sound of this kid's voice. If ever there was a time in my life I wish I could have disappeared, that was the moment. A hot flash of embarrassment shot through me like a bolt of lightning as I sprinted through the yard to a clump of bushes across the street. My heart was pounding so fast, it felt as if it were about to leap from my chest. A cool breeze blew across my bare legs and lifted the bottom of the dress as I attempted to run to seclusion.

It wasn't long before my makeshift hiding place was discovered by two acquaintances and several curious spectators eagerly searching for this freaked-out boy wearing a blue dress.

"Look! Kevin's wearing a dress!" Roars of laughter echoed through the neighborhood as the boisterous crowd chased me down in an attempt to catch a glimpse of the little boy in drag.

"Hey, kid, why do you have a dress on?" asked a man working in the yard next to where I was hiding. What was there to say? Should I admit the fact that I wet the bed? Or say I was a sissy and had this sick inner desire to be a little girl? As I replayed these thoughts in my mind, I frantically ran into the woods and sat motionless in a thicket for several hours to escape the embarrassment.

It was just about dark when fear drove me out of the woods and back to the house. I ran up the stairs and into my room, where I immediately ripped the tattered, grass-stained dress from my body and threw it to the floor.

Needless to say, from that day on, I never wet the bed again.

Gingerbread Cottage

Chapter 10

Illumination Night

*I*t was early evening on the third Wednesday of August, 1962. And, as the sun sank behind the treetops at the back of the cemetery across the street, a reddish orange hue faded below the horizon, marking the transition to dusk. Dinner was over, the kitchen had been cleaned up, and the dishes were put away. A subtle energy flowed through the air in the house because it was Illumination Night in Oak Bluffs, and we kids could hardly contain our excitement. Anticipation was heightened by thoughts of walking down to the Campground after dark to take part in this festive event.

Illumination Night, also known as Grand Illumination, is an annual celebration featuring both the display of Japanese lanterns throughout the Campground and also live entertainment at the Tabernacle. This tradition began in 1869, when a real estate developer, Erastus Payson Carpenter, attended a Methodist camp meeting on Martha's Vineyard in what used to be known as Wesleyan Grove (later renamed Cottage City). When the camp meeting was over, Mr. Carpenter took up residence at a cottage in the Campground for two years. He was later credited with being a catalyst in the incorporation of the town of Oak Bluffs in 1907.

Every year since, residents of the gingerbread cottages adorned them with fancy decorations and colorful lanterns hung from porches, eves, and rooftops. This one-night event created the epitome of an enchanted village, and spectators walked the narrow, winding streets and pathways to admire the friendly competition of creativity that took place among the neighbors. Since its inception, Illumination Night has grown in popularity and attracted more participants with each succeeding year.

⟿

I was upstairs rummaging through a knotted pile of clothes— looking for a decent shirt to wear—when I heard a shout come from the kitchen.

"Come on, you all; let's go. We don't want to be late."

After hearing the screen door close, I sensed I was mere minutes from being left behind, so I threw on a t-shirt and ran downstairs into the yard as fast as I could. When I got there, Nana was talking to my siblings, cousins, and a few other kids from the neighborhood, all of whom were giving her their undivided attention.

"Make sure you all stay together, behave yourselves, and be home no later than 10:30," Nana said.

It was almost dark by the time we were ready to go, and the streetlight at the entrance to the driveway—a single amber light bulb hanging under a metal fixture—flickered as it began to light up. We left the yard, ran past the darkened elementary school, and started down School Street.

Streetlights hanging from telephone poles made bright white circles of light on the pavement directly under them. It made us feel as if we were on stage in the gaze of a spotlight, visible while under it, but hidden by darkness the moment we stepped out of the light. The chirping of crickets imitated violins being bowed and plucked during an orchestral rendition of classical music, and tiny fireflies darted among the bushes and trees, blinking to the rhythm of the night, as we made our way toward the festivities.

Continuing down the street, we crossed Dukes County Avenue and made our way to the entrance of the Campground, the jovial sounds of music, singing, and laughter becoming louder as we got closer. When we arrived, throngs of people of all ages, ethnicities, and backgrounds were melded together, a tapestry of color that stretched across lawns and through the narrow streets.

The Tabernacle, usually a quiet place, had come to life. Soft white lights were strung around the lower edge of the roof of the iron structure, giving it the appearance of a carousel. Every seat inside the Tabernacle was occupied, and an orchestra played various selections of popular and classical music from the stage. Crowds of spectators sat on benches and on the grass to listen to the performance, joyfully singing along.

The gingerbread cottages were so beautifully decorated, they almost looked good enough to eat. One particular cottage stood out from the rest, though. It was painted in bright shades of pink and purple and resembled a large dollhouse. The colors were so vivid, you could easily have imagined it being a giant gingerbread cookie trimmed with gumdrops and a sugary white frosting. The grass on the front lawn of this cottage was so lush, it looked artificial—as if it could have been used to line the inside of an Easter basket full of decorated eggs and chocolate bunnies.

Street vendors pushed their carts and displayed their wares, which were snatched up almost faster than they could be replaced. Balloons, streamers, and other novelties were everywhere, and the whole experience was akin to a Mardi Gras celebration. The mood was festive, and everyone you met was smiling from ear to ear. Any attempt to avoid being swept away by the intoxication of the moment was futile, for the magic in the air cast a spell impossible to overcome.

During the festivities, we had no problem staying together, except for the occasional wandering around or temporarily getting lost in the crowd, which was expected. If we did get separated, we always knew to go directly to the Tabernacle to reconnect.

Every year on Illumination Night, we walked the grounds, admired the lanterns on display, then went home. This particular year, however, was different; the irresistible pull of temptation had grabbed hold of a couple of us. Instead of going back to the house empty-handed, we found ourselves in possession of three uniquely shaped and colorful crepe paper Japanese lanterns that had not been given to any of us.

We had stolen them.

While walking up School Street on our way back to the house, we desperately tried to think of a viable story to tell Nana about how we obtained these decorative ornaments with no money. If she was to detect the slightest flaw in our story, that would seal our fate and guarantee a painful beating for all of us.

"What should we say to Nana about these lanterns?" Chuck asked.

"Let's tell her we found them on the ground," Charlene said.

"Yeah, right. Do you *really* think she'll go for that?" Vincent asked.

Joanne made it clear she didn't want to know where they came from. Becky, Charlene's friend, said, "Maybe we should just throw them away and not take any chances."

"Are you out of your mind? After all the trouble we went through to get these lanterns? We're bringing them home," Carmella said.

A somber silence fell over us as we continued to walk. When we reached the top of the street and started down the sandy slope toward the house, we felt the tension as a result of our indecision about whether we should go forward with a story, or play it safe and abandon the lanterns while we still had our asses intact.

It was 10:30, and the moment of truth had arrived. Nana was peering out the kitchen window as we opened the door.

"Hi, Nana, we're back—right on time," Joanne said.

"Yes, I see. Did everyone have a good time?" Nana asked.

"We sure did. It was crowded, and the lanterns and decorations were beautiful!" Becky responded.

"What's that you have there?" Nana asked, with a curious expression on her face.

"Umm . . . a man said we could have these lanterns because they were damaged and were going to be thrown away," Vincent explained.

A deafening silence fell over the room as Nana processed what she had just heard. At that moment, time seemed to stand still. Although the lull lasted only a few seconds, it felt as if it were an eternity. Nana turned around and reached for one of the lanterns. She held it up to the light and slowly rotated the colorful crepe paper ornament to inspect it. The silence was finally broken when she said, "These will look good in the living room."

Our mouths dropped open in disbelief as we breathed a sigh of relief. We were going to live to see another day.

Those three lanterns remained proudly suspended from our grandmother's living room ceiling for many years. Long after she had passed away, there they hung—faded, torn, and dusty—up until the time the house was burned to the ground at the hands of an arsonist in 1994.

Kevin and the old shed next door

Chapter 11

Old Shed Next Door

A small cottage once stood approximately twenty feet from my grandmother's house. It was a simple wooden structure that looked more like an oversized shed than an actual cottage. Its old cedar shingles were cracked and broken, and many had fallen to the ground due to the weathering effects of the elements.

There was something mysterious about that building. I do not recall seeing anyone go into or come out of it; the windows and doors were tightly boarded up. Year after year, it remained unoccupied and devoid of any activity, and it gradually deteriorated as the wooden frame holding up the fragile structure rotted away. Shingles fell from the exterior walls like leaves from a deciduous tree in autumn, and those on the roof blew off with the slightest gust of the wind.

For some reason, Nana was overly protective of that shed and often went out of her way to keep us from going anywhere near it; she always warned us to stay away, with threats of getting whacked with the strap. If we so much as thought about disobey-ing her directive, or were foolish enough to be caught snooping around the shed, a stern reprimand was promptly administered.

There were times I heard strange noises coming from the shed, which drew me closer to it, but, each time that happened, the sound of Nana's voice echoed in my mind and stopped me in my tracks. As it turned out, those noises were only a by-product of the natural decaying process, caused by beams falling down, shin-gles dropping off, plywood warping, and floors and roof buckling.

The owner of the property remained anonymous to us kids, and Nana steadfastly refrained from offering any clues as to who it was. This enigma was too much for a bunch of inquisitive grandchil-dren to bear, and made us determined to unravel the mystery of what the *real* deal was with this place. Was it a hideout for some person or persons trying to evade the law? Did it contain money or valuables illegally acquired through a bank heist or some other crime? Perhaps there was a dead body buried under the rubble inside, its spirit condemned to haunt the place for all eternity. We were full of juvenile suppositions and conspiracy theories.

The shed sat directly across from Nana's house, and every time I peeked at it through my tiny bedroom window when the moon was full on a cloudless night, a silvery glow illuminated the dark, lifeless structure, casting shadows that became optical illusions.

Its eerie appearance was similar to that of a haunted house on Halloween. Some nights, bats sporadically darted about the shed and scooped up mosquitoes in midair, their fluttering wings—reflecting the light of the moon—flashing in the night sky. This impromptu light show spooked me and made me jump back into my musty bed to hide under the sheets. As I lay there,

visions of the supernatural crept into my thoughts while I rest-
lessly attempted to force myself to sleep.

Not long after I drifted off one night, the blaring sound of
the fire alarm on the roof of the downtown fire station pierced
the still of the night and abruptly awakened me. My body
shook with fear. The alarm was so loud, it sounded as if it were
on top of my grandmother's house. The intermittent shrill—a
patterned series of disturbing siren blasts—repeated again and
again. Its purpose was to designate the location of a fire and
alert the volunteer fire department to mobilize their resources
so they could extinguish the flames.

In a semiconscious state, I wondered if our house was on
fire. Or could the shed next door have been set ablaze? After
all, it *was* a withered and dry old building—a perfect tinderbox.
Finally determining that neither our house nor the shed next
door was on fire, I lay back down and waited for the noise to
subside, and eventually fell asleep again.

The following morning, I crawled across my bed to look out
the window and check on the shed. Had it actually succumbed
to the events of the previous night, or had I just had a bad
dream? I peered through the window and there it stood—quiet,
abandoned, and as rickety as ever—being dismantled only
slowly and by the passage of time.

Over the years, our faulty conspiracy theories were peeled
away like the layers of an onion; none had a basis in fact. We
were left with having to accept that old shed as being nothing
more than a place where our grandmother attached one end of
a clothesline and stored the garbage cans for the Monday and
Thursday trash pickup. The only signs of life I ever saw at the

shed were rabbits, skunks, snakes, and swarms of hornets that had built nests under the eaves.

Every summer, wild grasses grew to about three feet high around the shed and made it appear as if it were situated in a field of golden shoots reaching up toward the bright blue sky. Whenever we walked through the grass that surrounded the shed, it almost felt as if we were on a safari, expecting to see an elephant or a zebra meander by at any time.

After years of neglect, the shed inevitably succumbed to the elements and completely fell apart. First, the roof caved in, allowing the wind, rain, and snow to compromise further the integrity of the weak structure. Next, a wall collapsed, followed by another, in a manner similar to the flaps of a cardboard box being folded closed.

Once the walls were no longer standing, the interior of the shed was exposed, revealing the imagined secrets kept hidden inside all those years. Among the pile of rubble in the building were remnants of what had been two small rooms and a bath-room. There was no sign of money, dead bodies, or ghosts—only splintered pieces of an old withered building that had somehow lost its owner, its identity, and its very existence after being subjected to many years of abandonment.

The old shed next door was reduced to a mound of sawdust and rusty nails that were eventually swept away by gale force winds howling across the island like a runaway locomotive.

Although our thirst for answers about this once-mysterious structure had been quenched by its destruction, we still felt a sense of loss at the passing of this inanimate object—one that had created a sense of wonder and intrigue to stimulate our young imaginations for so many years.

Chapter 12

Clamming and Crabbing

*M*y siblings, cousins, and I enjoyed a variety of outdoor pursuits during our summers on the Vineyard. They usually involved simple activities that might have been boring or mundane to other youngsters, but to us—from modest means and unable to do things that required money—these outings were always adventurous and fun. Perhaps we simply didn't know any better, but, as I reflect, I feel a sense of gratitude for those cherished times in our lives. Fond remembrances still stir joyful emotions.

Clamming and crabbing were two of our favorite things to do because they contained elements of both sport and leisure. It was sport to dig for clams buried beneath the sand in shallow water, or trap nimble crabs with a net before they scurried away and hid between submerged rocks. But it was a leisure activity, too, because we were required to get physically into the water and walk slowly through it while searching for sweet mollusks and tasty crustaceans.

After catching them, we brought them home to be cooked, then served over a bed of steamed rice with, on the side, a golden ear of corn heavily salted and dripping with melted oleomargarine. Back then, it was easy for us to catch something to bring home, and the reward of enjoying the meal at the end of the day made the whole activity much more satisfying.

We often went to dig for clams at Sengekontacket Pond, across the road from Joseph A. Sylvia State Beach, just beyond the second bridge. Nestled between the towns of Oak Bluffs and Edgartown, Sengekontacket Pond was a large body of water covering an area of about two-and-one-half square miles. Sheltered and shallower than the open ocean, it provided a safe haven for less daring souls to practice their sailing or fishing skills in more tranquil waters.

On three small islands in the middle of the pond, piping plovers, terns, and an assortment of other birds found refuge and a place to nest undisturbed by humans and natural predators. When the sun began to set, the tranquil water in the pond reflected a magenta-colored sky and clouds resembling wispy puffs of pink cotton candy. This environment made you feel as if you were a little closer to God, while, at the same time, intoxicated by the miraculous wonders of nature. It was always peaceful and picturesque at the pond, and it was easy to be lulled into a hypnotic trance.

Our crabbing activities took place down the street, opposite the Bend-in-the-Road Beach in Edgartown. We usually rode our bikes to get there, but, whenever we had the luxury of being driven by car, our catch was much greater because we were able to bring the buckets, nets, and shovels we needed to snag and haul back clams and crabs.

One vibrant summer's day, we waited patiently in the backyard for Mr. Norris, who was coming over to take us to Sengekontacket Pond for an afternoon of clamming and crabbing. While waiting, Chuck and Vincent took an inventory of items that we planned to take with us.

"Five nets?"

"Check."

"Three buckets?"

"Check."

"Three small shovels?"

"Check."

"Two fishing poles?"

"Check."

"Bait?"

"What?"

"Bait! You know—squid."

"Oh, yeah; check."

"Two pair of goggles?"

"Check."

"Six beach towels?"

"Check."

"Rubber boots?"

"Check."

"Looks like we have everything," Chuck said.

"Yep, looks like we do," Vincent answered.

Within minutes, Mr. Norris arrived. After tossing our items into the trunk, we piled into his car in our usual haphazard fashion, drove down Pacific Avenue, and made a left turn onto Vineyard Avenue. We then took a right on Dukes County, an immediate left onto Masonic, and proceeded across Circuit Avenue past the tennis courts and around Waban Park. Finally, we made another right on to Sea View Avenue, which ran parallel to the Inkwell, a small beach. Nantucket Sound was to our left, just beyond the seawall.

All the while we motored toward State Beach and Edgartown, we enthusiastically discussed how excited we were to be going clamming and crabbing—and we didn't pass up any opportunities to tease each other.

"I'll bet that I catch more crabs than anyone," Vincent proclaimed.

"No way, Vincent," Carmella replied. "I can catch more than you in my sleep."

"Well, Carmella, as soon as you wake up from that dream you're apparently having right now, you'll see that you don't know what you're talking about," Vincent countered.

"We shall see," Carmella said.

"Yes, we will," Vincent answered.

"I'm going to catch the most clams," I said with confidence.

"Kevin, please. You'll be lucky to get just one," Chuck said.

"Shut up, Chucky. I've been going clamming since before you were born."

"What are you talking about, Kevin? I'm five years older than you are!" Chuck said.

"So what? I'm still going to catch more than you," I said.

"All right, you all. Stop that bickering back there," Nana said.

The bright afternoon sun bounced off the water as calm ocean currents carried small waves gently to the shore. Continuing past Harthaven and the Farm Neck Golf Course, the winding, two-lane road became a straightaway. Cars of beachgoers were parked along the side of the road, and we could see umbrellas swaying in the wind through tall stands of beach grass growing on the sand dunes. As soon as we crossed the second bridge, Mr. Norris pulled the car onto a sandy shoulder at the pond. It was low tide, and conditions were perfect for clamming.

"Let's go catch some clams and crabs!" he said.

We hopped out of the car, grabbed our gear from the trunk, and walked to the edge of the pond. There we dropped everything on to the ground. Then, with nets, buckets, and shovels in hand, we slowly waded into the warm mud- and sand-bottomed pond, carefully looking for the telltale sign of a clam buried beneath the sand—a stream of air bubbles rising to the surface.

"I see some bubbles over here," Charlene said.

We all ran over to confirm her claim.

"Dig, Charlene, dig!" Mr. Norris yelled.

Charlene plunged her shovel into the wet sand several times with all her might and, seconds later, scooped up a big fat clam.

"I got it!" she said with excitement, as she brushed the sand off and dropped the clam into the bucket.

"Good job! Okay, kids, Charlene caught the first clam. Let's see what the rest of us can do," Mr. Norris said.

We fanned out across the area to search for more clams, poking and prodding at every bubble that rose to the surface of the wet sand. We caught thirty-six clams and several quahogs in two-and-one-half hours.

When the bucket was full, we covered the catch with ocean water and carried it back to the car where Nana was sitting. Almost immediately, she picked a quahog from the bucket and carefully pried it open with a knife. With great anticipation,

Nana removed the slimy innards from its shell and slid them down her throat.

"*Eeeew*, Nana! How can you eat those things raw like that?" I asked.

"They're tasty and good for you, too. Would you like to try one?"

"No, thanks, but I'd bet that seagull over there will take you up on your offer."

She smiled, grabbed another one, and gobbled it down.

After catching as many clams as we could carry back with us, we packed up our gear and drove one mile down the road to hunt for crabs.

At the Bend-in-the-Road Beach, a small stream flowed under the pavement and emptied into the pond. On both sides of the inlet, the banks were supported by large rocks among which crabs were known to congregate in water about two-feet deep.

Because crabs are cunning little creatures, catching them requires the use of strategic planning. They move sideways at a rapid pace and never give in without a fight; they are not shy about going on the offensive, and are known to attack your feet, legs, or hands with a nip of their sharp claws. Each time we ventured into the water to look for crabs, we had to be vigilant or would surely suffer from the painful effects of their aggression.

Our crabbing strategy went something like this: two of us grabbed a fishing pole, baited the hook with a small piece of squid, and lowered it into the water near the rocks to lure the crabs out of hiding. The rest of us carefully waded into the water with our nets in hand and waited for the crabs to go after the bait. Once they went for the bait, we scooped them up with a net and dropped them into a bucket. For every few crabs we attempted to catch, we were lucky to trap any of them because they moved fast and often got away.

After climbing down the embankment and onto the rocks at the water's edge, Mr. Norris surveyed the area and waved to us to come down.

"Kevin, bring the fishing poles over here so I can put some bait on the hooks," Mr. Norris said.

I threw the poles over my shoulder and took them with me as instructed. Mr. Norris cut off two pieces of squid, threaded them onto the hooks, and handed one pole to Joanne and the other to Charlene.

"Okay, kids, here's what I want you to do. Stand on this rock right here and lower the bait into the water next to those submerged boulders. Then slowly move the poles from side to side while dragging the bait along the bottom."

"Like this?" Charlene asked.

"Yes, but not so fast. You want the crabs to see the bait and come out after it," he replied.

"Charlene, it's kind of like waving a baton, but in slow motion," Joanne said.

"Joanne's got it," Mr. Norris said, causing a wide grin to appear on her face.

"Give me a net; I see a crab!" Vincent said.

"Chuck, Carmella, Vincent, Kevin—grab a net and wade into the water. When you get near the bait, I want you to stand completely still," Mr. Norris instructed.

We complied with his directive, and Vincent attempted to catch the crab he had seen by swiping at it with his net. However, it quickly retreated under the rocks.

"Darn it!" he said with frustration.

"Like I told you before, you have to outsmart the crabs. They aren't going to just jump into your nets and be hauled off for your next meal," Mr. Norris said.

With nets in hand, we positioned ourselves in the shallow water and stood completely still. Nana was clearly amused as she watched us trying to imitate a small flock of storks standing motionless in the pond, patiently waiting for the next meal to swim by.

"Hey, you guys, get ready. The crabs are starting to go after the bait," Charlene said.

"We know; we see them," Vincent replied.

Before long, a small army of crabs were marching toward the bait, fighting among themselves for the pieces of squid on the hooks. We waited for just the right moment to ambush the unsuspecting crustaceans.

"Get them!" Carmella screamed.

The sounds of us splashing through the water and dragging our nets along the bottom quickly replaced the relative calm that had existed just moments before. We pounced and attempted to scoop them up with our nets before they scattered back to safety under the rocks.

"I have two crabs in my net!" Chuck proudly said.

"I got one! Carmella said.

"I caught one, too!" Vincent said.

At that point, I had not caught any crabs, but, when I heard Vincent proudly proclaim that he had caught one, I was determined to catch one, too. After several attempts, I still came up empty-netted. Noticing my frustration, Charlene, in her usual compassionate manner, said, "Kev, I'll help you catch a crab."

She repositioned her fishing pole and placed the baited hook in the water next to me, moving it back and forth to lure the crabs out of hiding. Shortly thereafter, the hungry crabs reemerged from under the rocks and made a beeline for the bait. As luck—along with a little help from my cousin—would have it, I not only caught a crab, but, much to my delight, I snagged three of them.

Our final tally was twenty-two crabs that afternoon, and, when we added those to the clams caught earlier, there was enough shellfish for quite a feast that evening.

Chapter 13

The Blueberry Boys

While lounging in the backyard on a stifling hot summer afternoon, I felt a refreshing breeze suddenly kick up from the northwest. Above me, a bright, multicolored umbrella—it reminded me of a roll of candy Lifesavers—swayed back and forth as it resisted becoming airborne when strong gusts of wind attempted to lift it as if it were a parachute. The splintered wooden pole supporting the umbrella rattled against its broken-down table, old and faded and with red paint chips peeling off it.

I peered through the screen door and looked at the clock on the wall. Its hands seemed to be frozen as another day replayed itself, like a summer rerun on television.

"What do you all feel like doing today?" Vincent asked.

"I don't know. Maybe I'll go see if Howie is at home," Chuck said.

"It's hot outside; I'd like to go to the beach," I said.

"Why do you want to go to the beach? You can't even swim," Vincent said.

"Yes, I can!"

"No, you can't."

"Can, too!"

"You cannot."

"Shut up, Vincent!" I said.

"Vincent, leave Kevin alone," Joanne said, abruptly interrupting our exchange.

"He knows he doesn't know how to swim," Vincent said, in defense of his badgering.

"So what? He's younger than you. Leave him alone!" Joanne repeated, getting the last word.

"Let's go over to the orchard and pick some apples," Charlene suggested.

"Nah. It's too hot over there. How about going into the woods to pick some blueberries, blackberries, and strawberries? Maybe Nana will make us a pie if we get enough of them," Carmella said.

"That's a good idea, Carmella," Vincent responded.

Chuck, Joanne, and Charlene also agreed with the idea, so it appeared we had a consensus in support of going berry picking.

"I'll ask Nana if we can go," Carmella said.

As she ran to the door to ask, Nana's stout figure suddenly appeared in the doorway.

"Nana, can we go into the woods to pick some berries?" Carmella asked.

"I don't know if you all should go by yourselves," Nana said.

"Why not?" we asked simultaneously.

"Well, if you must know, I'm afraid the Blueberry Boys will get you," Nana replied.

The Blueberry Boys

"The Blueberry Boys? Who are the Blueberry Boys?" we asked.

Nana began her explanation and we listened intently, but with suspicion.

"The Blueberry Boys are a bunch of kids who live in the woods; they have no parents and hide out in the forest. I've heard they guard all the fruit and berries that grow there, and that several children—about your age—went into the woods and were never seen again. I don't want that to happen to you kids," she said.

We all looked at each other while attempting to gauge the believability of Nana's story. Because I was the youngest and most gullible, I envisioned these boys as a pack of wild animals roaming through the forest, terrorizing everything in its path.

"That's a bunch of malarkey!" Vincent said.

Chuck's facial expression made it clear it was the most ridiculous story he had ever heard. The girls had semiblank expressions on their faces, making it difficult to discern what they thought.

Nana then continued, "But, if you all still want to go, be careful and don't let them catch you."

Vincent encouraged us by saying, "Let's go! Don't believe that story about the Blueberry Boys."

"All right, but don't say I didn't warn you," she said, with a serious tone.

Nana left the doorway and soon returned with three wicker picnic baskets to use to collect the berries.

"Thanks, Nana. We'll be back a little later," Joanne said.

We left the house, crossed the street, and walked through the cemetery to the edge of the woods in back. There a row of tall scrub pine, oak, and maple trees welcomed us with their intimidating presence. Thick stands of bushes and plants grew randomly from the floor of the forest, along with countless varieties of flowers, grasses, and trees. I had never seen so many variations of flora in my life.

We followed a path of dirt and pine needles that led us deep into the dark woods, and the cemetery suddenly disappeared from sight. Through the tops of the leaf-filled trees, the blue sky was barely visible, and an eerie shade was cast over the entire forest. Shadows moved sporadically amongst the dense foliage, and scary thoughts provoked illusions that fed the fear of our young imaginations.

As we continued down the winding path, we spotted the first blueberry bush, followed by many more, all loaded with plump, juicy berries—ripe and ready to be picked.

"There's a blueberry bush!" Carmella yelled.

"Here's another one, and another!" Joanne said.

We descended upon the blueberry bushes like seagulls diving down on a school of fish, and, in no time, we picked them clean, filling our baskets with the luscious fruit. Just beyond the blueberries were bushels of strawberries and blackberries that seemed to call out to us to come and harvest them. We couldn't resist the urge to pop some of the berries into our mouths as we picked, and the sweet, dark juice stained our lips and tongues blue and black as we gulped them down.

Before long, our baskets were overflowing with more berries than we knew what to do with. Pleased with the bounty we were about to take home, we sent chants of jubilation echoing throughout the forest while skipping down the path as if we were in a scene from the movie, *The Wizard of Oz:* "Strawberries, blueberries, blackberries, oh my! Strawberries, blueberries, blackberries, oh my!"

As we attempted to find our way back out of the woods, a strange rustling sound came from the underbrush just off the path in front of us—and stopped us in our tracks.

"Did you hear that?" Charlene asked.

"Shhh, be quiet," Vincent said, as he slowly crept toward the area he thought the sound came from. Without warning, something leaped out of a bush, and Vincent screamed, "It's the Blueberry Boys! Run!"

We scattered in different directions and ran through the woods, off the beaten path, unsure of which way would lead us back to the cemetery.

Joanne and Charlene each grabbed one of my hands and dragged me along with them. As we stumbled our way through the brush, our arms and legs were scratched by the whipping action of thickets and tree branches. Carmella, Chuck, and Vincent, running with the baskets of berries, dropped half of them on the ground as they followed each other, screaming as loud as they could.

"Hey, you guys! Where are you?" we called out to them.

"Over here!" we heard them yell. Panting and nearly out of breath, we kept running, following the sound of their voices until we finally caught up with them.

"Are you guys all right?" Joanne asked.

"Yeah," Chuck said.

"I'm scared! Let's get the heck out of here," Charlene said.

I was so frightened, my mouth was as dry as a desert breeze, and my tongue was lodged in the back of my throat, making it impossible for me to utter a sound.

"Vincent, what did you see?" Carmella asked.

"I really don't know, but, whatever it was, it moved fast and I wasn't about to stick around to find out!"

Beyond the frayed nerves, a few cuts and scratches, and some lost berries, we all appeared to be okay.

"Where is the cemetery?" Charlene asked.

"I think it's over that way. Follow me," my brother replied.

Chuck's Boy Scout experience came in handy, and, after more wandering through the woods, we suddenly found ourselves at the edge of the cemetery. Relieved to have finally made it out of the woods, we ran back to our grandmother's house with the berries. When we entered the kitchen, Nana asked, "How did the berry picking go?"

"Great!" Vincent responded, as he, Chuck, and Carmella placed their baskets on the table.

Nana inspected the baskets. "You all collected quite a few berries, but I see that the baskets are only half full. What happened?" Nana asked.

"We would have brought back more berries, but we had an accident and dropped some of them on the ground," Vincent explained.

"I should be able to make two or three pies with these," Nana said.

After Vincent heard that, he started to smile, and said, "I told you there was no such thing as the Blueberry Boys, Nana."

The rest of us gawked at him as if he had completely lost his mind. Our grandmother carried the baskets over to the sink where she separated the leaves, twigs, and stems from the berries before rinsing them off—the first step to their becoming the main ingredient of her delicious, golden-crust pies.

Sam, Chuck, and Carmella

Chapter 14

Bicycling

*T*he only form of transportation we had as kids on Martha's Vineyard—beyond the occasional car ride—was the bicycle.

I was fortunate to have with me my gold, three-speed bicycle—complete with reflectors, head- and taillights, chrome handlebars, beige handgrips, and a battery-operated horn. My trusty bike took me just about everywhere on the island, allowing me to explore places other kids never even considered going. As I recall, on only one street in Oak Bluffs were bikes restricted from traveling, and that was downtown on Circuit Avenue. Cars and pedestrians created so much congestion; adding bikes to the mix would only have exacerbated the chaos and the potential for injury.

Every summer, I accumulated a significant amount of mileage on my bike—day after day and week after week—so it was imperative that it be kept in good working order. Any mainte-nance or minor repairs were funded by money earned from coin diving (see chapter 18), and I religiously put some of it away for such things, stashed in an old sock I kept under my bed at Nana's house.

Biking around the Vineyard was an activity that began in our family when my mother and her siblings spent time there as teenagers in the 1930s. By the time my brother, sisters, cousins, and I began visiting the island in the late 1950s and early '60s, bicycling was still an adventure because bike paths were non-existent back then. We were in God's hands as we cycled over main streets and thoroughfares, up and down winding roads, through fields and forests, and to the beaches. Not only did we ride on just about every road, street, and path throughout Oak Bluffs, we fearlessly ventured to the neighboring towns of Vineyard Haven, Tisbury, West Tisbury, Edgartown, and Chilmark. On a few occasions, we even made it all the way out to Gay Head and back, a trip which took us all day.

One afternoon, while sitting in the backyard staring at my bike as it stood upright on its kickstand, I happened to notice my cousin Vincent opening the door from the kitchen to come outside. That is when the thought hit me.

"Do you feel like taking a ride to Vineyard Haven to watch the ferry come in?" I asked.

"Sure," he replied.

"We'd better ask Nana if we can go. I don't want to get yelled at or whacked with the strap," I said.

"You're right. I'll go ask her now."

Vincent walked back into the house where he found Nana

My mother on a bike—1941

sitting at the kitchen table playing a game of Solitaire with a cold can of Narragansett beer next to her. He stood and waited for the right moment to ask because he didn't want to interrupt her card game. While waiting, Vincent briefly focused his attention on the can of beer and watched the tiny drops of condensation slowly slide down the side of the can like tears flowing over a face. Nana paused for a moment to reach for the beer, but, before picking it up, she wrapped a napkin around it to insulate her hand from the chilled can before taking a sip. His moment to ask had arrived.

"Nana, is it okay for Kevin and me to ride our bikes to Vineyard Haven and watch the ferry come in?"

She slowly placed the can back on the table and peered over the top of her eyeglasses. Looking squarely at Vincent, she pondered for a moment, then said, "You can go, but watch out for the traffic."

"We will," he replied.

When Vincent emerged from the house, I could tell by his wide grin that our request had been granted. In no time, we hopped onto our bikes and made our way up the grassy slope of the driveway and on to Pacific Avenue. Riding parallel to each other, my cousin and I verbally mapped out the route to get to Vineyard Haven.

"Let's go the back way and take Vineyard Avenue to County Road; we can then ride down Beach Road to the drawbridge and along the harbor to the dock. There will be less traffic that way," Vincent suggested.

"Okay. Sounds good to me," I replied.

When we reached Vineyard Avenue, we made a right turn.

Bicycling

Vincent took the lead, and I followed him as we passed by
Sacred Heart Cemetery, a small, but well-maintained graveyard surrounded by a white post-and-beam fence. A little
farther down the street—just before County Road—was the
Holy Ghost Association, an organization founded by people
of Portuguese decent. A number of cultural events were held
there throughout the summer, including the annual Portuguese Feast. Turning on to County Road, we cycled past
the Martha's Vineyard Hospital and then on to Beach Road,
which led us to the drawbridge.

Although we had made the same trip countless times before,
this time was going to be different, though we didn't know it yet.

The narrow road leading to the drawbridge required us to
navigate up a steep incline to reach the top. To scale the bridge
successfully, we had to build up enough speed to counteract
the force of gravity that slowed the bike down as it climbed the
hill. I was impressed by my ability to reach a speed that not only
pushed my bike up the hill with ease, but also created momen-
tum to carry me over the top of the bridge.

I followed closely behind my cousin as we crested the highest
point on the bridge and barreled down the other side of the
slope. For some reason, Vincent stopped his bike at the bottom
of the hill. Not paying attention, I did not look up until I was
only seconds from rear-ending him, and, in a panic, I squeezed
the front brake handle instead of the one that controlled the
rear brakes. The cumulative forces of speed, inattention, and
the wrong reflexive response caused a chain reaction that
resulted in my being hurled headfirst over the handlebars.

With my arms extended out in front of me, I closed my eyes

and cringed as my body flew through the air and fell to the pavement. I skidded across the sandy asphalt, scraping the skin off my hands, elbows, and knees; the intense pain made me scream as the salty air cut into my sensitive nerve endings like a sharp razor. My bike fell to the ground, and Vincent jumped off his and ran over to me.

"Are you all right?" he asked.

Unable to answer him, I got up, brushed the sand off as best I could, and limped over to my bike to pick it up. In an attempt to control the discomfort and to hide the fact that I felt like a fool, I turned my attention to the harbor and noticed the ferry we were supposed to have met was already gliding over the water toward the dock.

Realizing we would not make it in time, we turned our bikes around and headed back to the house. When we got there, I gave our grandmother a lame explanation about what had happened, and, to minimize the embarrassment, I tried to make light of my own stupidity. After hearing my story, Nana went into the bathroom and got the hydrogen peroxide and cotton balls to disinfect the wounds before patching me up.

The very next morning, I was up and on my bike again, heading for the water's edge to indulge myself in the medicinal qualities of the ocean. I remember Nana telling me that salt water helped speed up the healing process, and I didn't hesitate to take advantage of it. That advice proved to be true; my scrapes and scratches began to look much better after being treated with the cool ocean water.

Bicycling

Later that day, five of us cousins were sitting around in the yard planning an evening bike ride through select parts of Oak Bluffs, an activity we often engaged in.

"I think we should ride through the Campground and then over to Ocean Park; from there, let's follow New York Avenue past the harbor and go to the East Chop Lighthouse," I suggested. "What do you all think?"

"If we're going to do that, we had better make sure we're back before Nana gets home from work," Chuck said.

"East Chop Drive is dangerous, especially at night—you know there are no streetlights up there—and, with that winding road near the cliff, we might accidentally fall over the edge," Vincent said.

"Chucky, which do you think would be worse? Falling off the cliff or getting a beating from Nana?" Carmella asked.

"What kind of ridiculous question is that?" Chuck asked.

"What do you mean, Chucky?

"What I *mean* is, why would you ask such a stupid question?"

"I don't know, but I'd take the cliff over Nana's whooping," Carmella joked.

"I'm not surprised," Vincent said. "If I got as many beatings as you do, Carmella, I'd probably take the cliff, too. We all know you're the queen when it comes to getting a beating."

"Shut up, Vincent!"

"Carmella, you know it's true," Charlene said.

"No, it's not! Chucky gets whipped just as much as I do," Carmella said.

"No, I don't, Carmella. Like Vincent just said, you are THE QUEEN!" Chuck responded.

"Well, if I'm the queen, then let it be known that you *certainly* must be the king!"

It was just after dark and we were ready to go. Nana was at work, and the six of us were free to do as we pleased. We jumped onto our bikes, pedaled up to the beginning of the driveway, and quickly made it over to School Street. Looking down the steep hill, we took off, one after the other, increasing our speed in a matter of seconds. The rush we felt as our bikes sped along, the wind whipping across our faces, gave us a sense of freedom and invincibility.

Within minutes, we entered the Campground and followed the circular drive where many of the quaint and colorful gingerbread cottages were closely tucked together. As expected, all was quiet there; the only thing we saw were faint white lights filtering through the windows of the cottages. There was no activity outside—except for us, who had every intention of livening up the place with our youthful presence.

Our bikes rolled over the narrow, bumpy street and rattled on the knobs and imperfections in the road, jarring our bodies as we rode through the grounds. The tranquility of the evening was disrupted by the sound of our voices yelling at the top of our lungs while cycling through the neighborhood.

After circling the Tabernacle twice, our bikes began to roll faster and faster—almost as if we had been wound up like a big spring that was recoiled and released—launching us on a trajectory through the Campground and down a winding road that snaked between rows of tiny cottages. We dashed through the Campground, and, by the time any of the residents made it outside to investigate the source of the disturbance, we were long gone and on our way to Ocean Park.

Bicycling

Next we raced through an alley before crossing Circuit Avenue in front of Nick's Lighthouse. After navigating our way around cars and pedestrians, we rode our bikes up Kennebec Avenue and turned onto Healey Way, which led us to Ocean Park. Sweating and out of breath, we coasted down one of the paths in the park and stopped to rest at the bandstand. The six of us jumped off our bikes and sat down on the grass.

Couples were casually walking the grounds and conversing on benches. Everyone appeared to be enjoying the beautiful evening as invigorating ocean breezes flowed through the park and gently caressed us as we sat there catching our breaths.

I decided to lie down on my back, and, when I did, looked up into the night sky and felt a sense of wonderment. I was moved by the sight of thousands of stars with varying intensities of light, twinkling like miniature diamonds suspended from a dark velvet ceiling. The Milky Way galaxy, with its billions of stars and clouds of cosmic dust, streaked across the sky above us with the brilliance of a comet. A soft, yellow crescent moon hung just above the horizon, faintly illuminating the ocean beneath it.

"Hey, I can see the Big Dipper," Charlene said.

"Where?" Carmella asked.

"Right over there."

"Over where? There are a gazillion stars up there; how can you be sure?"

"It's as obvious as the big nose on your face. I'll point it out—one, two, three, four, five, six, and seven. Four stars make up the dipper, and three make up the handle," she explained.

"Oh, yeah, I see it now . . . look at that." We all just sat there entranced by the cosmos as we stared up into space.

"I hate to break up the astronomy lesson, but it's time to go, you all. If we want to make it back before Nana gets home, we'd better get going," Chuck said.

We picked up our bikes and ran alongside them, pushing them forward before jumping on the seats. After pedaling through the park, we proceeded down Oak Bluffs Avenue to the harbor and past Nancy's Snack Bar, where a row of pleasure boats were moored for the evening. As we zipped by, we saw people relaxing on the decks of the boats, partaking in drinks and socializing with friends from neighboring vessels, while others conversed with tourists strolling along the boardwalk and admiring the beautiful sights.

Upon reaching Our Market—a local convenience store on the far side of the harbor (formerly known as S.S. Pierce & Co.)—we made a right turn on to East Chop Drive. This narrow, two-lane road gradually went uphill before turning into a steep incline that required us to pedal in a stand-up position.

As we made our way up the dark road, the sound of the surf crashing on the rocks below reminded us how close we were to the edge of the cliff and warned us of the deadly drop lurking only a few feet away. When we reached the top of the hill, the road swerved gently to the left, and then to the right, bringing us to the East Chop Lighthouse.

This particular lighthouse—enclosed by a white picket fence—was unique in that it was painted a chocolate brown and displayed a flashing green light that faced Vineyard Haven Harbor and Vineyard Sound. From this vantage point on a clear evening, we could see the flickering white lights on Cape Cod, seven miles across the water.

We left the lighthouse and cycled down the road which

curved to the left at a blind corner before going downhill along the harbor. Out of nowhere, a car veered around the corner with its high beams on and nearly ran into us.

"Watch out!" we screamed.

Missing us by inches, the driver of the car laid on the horn as he swerved to avoid us and sped away.

"What the hell is wrong with that fool? He almost killed us!" Carmella snapped.

"I told you all it was dangerous up here in the dark," Vincent said.

"Let's just keep going; we can't let Nana beat us home," Chuck said.

"Chuck's right. Let's go," Joanne urged.

Not surprisingly, we were *all* shaken by almost being run over by that car. But we continued pedaling.

Minutes later, we approached a row of houses situated at the water's edge and purposely increased the distance between ourselves; we did not utter a sound as we rode past the green and white house where our grandmother worked as a cook. Having successfully made it past the house without being detected, we tightened up the formation and resumed our idle chatter.

"Did anyone see Nana through the kitchen window?" Carmella asked.

"Nah, I couldn't see anything. The white lace curtains hanging in the window blocked the view," Charlene said.

"That's a really nice house," Vincent noted.

"It sure is. I wonder what it looks like inside," Joanne asked.

"I'd bet that it's almost as luxurious as the mildew palace we stay at," Carmella said.

"Give me a break," Vincent replied.

We kept pedaling to the end of the street, which veered sharply to the left and then became New York Avenue. About a half mile up, we made a right turn on to Chestnut and then another right on to Pacific. Instead of going straight to the house, we followed each other through the Oak Grove Cemetery and zoomed up and down and around the perpendicular paths, hardly able to see each other in the dark of night. Eerie reflections bounced off the headstones, and the trees and their fluttering leaves created images of dark shadows as faint beams of moonlight filtered through them.

Finally, we left the cemetery, crossed the street, and pedaled down the driveway, single file, into the yard. After parking our bikes, we went into the house and felt a sense of relief knowing that our objective of bicycling around Oak Bluffs at night—and making it back before Nana got home from work—had been accomplished.

At ten o'clock on the dot, like clockwork, car lights appeared in the driveway as Nana's ride dropped her off at the house.

"Thanks for the ride. I'll see you tomorrow; have a good evening," she said, as she closed the car door.

Nana walked slowly across the yard, opened the screen door to the kitchen, and came inside.

"Hi, Nana. How was your night?" Joanne asked.

"My evening was fine. Did you all behave yourselves while I was at work?"

"Of course we did. It was a typical night for us; we just hung around like we always do."

Nana placed her purse on the table and hung her sweater

on a hook, then continued talking. "A funny thing happened on the way home tonight. We were driving through East Chop and almost hit a bunch of kids on bicycles. It was so dark; the driver couldn't see them until we were right on top of them. He complained about how those 'damn crazy kids' should have been at home that time of night. I agreed, and told him that *my* grandchildren would never have been out there riding around in the dark like they had lost their minds," she said.

Silence fell upon the room as we kids gave each other guilty glances, wondering if Nana really knew who those "damn crazy kids" were. If she did know, she gave no indication, which was very uncharacteristic of her—and very fortunate for us.

Chapter 15

Turbulent Times

*O*ne of the darkest and most turbulent times in modern
American history occurred over a ten-year period centered
in the 1960s. Four prominent American leaders were killed, the
civil rights movement came to a head, and our country was
fully engaged in the Vietnam War. A myriad of antiwar demonstrations and protests sprang up across the country, giving rise
to the burning of draft cards and the outright refusal to accept
what was perceived by many to be an unjust war.

In a bold attempt to address the issue of civil rights, a
small group of courageous black and white citizens initiated
a grassroots movement to rectify the injustice of segregation
in the south. Their goal was to ensure that America was a
place where "liberty and justice for all" was not a concept that
applied only to a select group of individuals, but that those
words actually had meaning that transcended race, and were
applicable to all citizens.

This new movement culminated in May 1961 when the inte-
grated group of civil rights activists—who called themselves the

Freedom Riders—openly challenged the status quo by placing black riders in seats at the front of a bus while another black person sat in a seat next to a white person, a clear violation of Jim Crow laws.

As they traveled through the south, one of the two buses was met with mob violence when it arrived in Anniston, Alabama, where it was firebombed with every intention of killing the occupants. These unprovoked attacks exposed the blatant disregard for the law of white segregationists, which forced the Kennedy administration to protect the civil rights of the Freedom Riders. This unprecedented move by the federal government proved to be a critical turning point in the eventual dismantling of Jim Crow laws in the south.

On November 22, 1963, President John F. Kennedy was assassinated while riding in a motorcade in Dallas, Texas; I was in the fourth grade at the time. I vividly remember my teacher, Miss Bees, tearfully dismissing our class and sending us home that Friday afternoon.

I did not fully understand the severity or historical significance of what had occurred, but, when I got home to find my mother sobbing in front of our black-and-white television set, a somber reality began to sink in. Observing the nonstop media coverage as the nation mourned this fallen president made me wonder—even at my young age—how such a horrific thing could happen in the United States.

The following year, on July 2, 1964, President Lyndon Johnson signed the Civil Rights Act into law which, in theory, ended segregation in public places and banned discriminatory practices in employment. Despite the enactment of this new law, most opportunities to earn a living through any dignified means continued to elude people of color, primarily because the Jim Crow mentality was alive and well, and still perpetuating the deprivation of economic upward mobility and social acceptance.

On February 21, 1965, Malcolm X, the charismatic black activist, was assassinated while giving a speech at the Audubon Ballroom in New York. The events leading up to this incident not only pitted black people against one another, but also fanned the flames of racial division in our country and sparked even more demands for equality by African Americans. The Black Power movement was steadily growing, and demonstrations became the norm throughout major urban areas in America.

In August of that same year, the Massachusetts state legislature passed the Racial Imbalance Act, which decreed that no school could have more than 50 percent nonwhite students enrolled. This legislative action gave rise to a court order which implemented forced busing to achieve integration. The intent was to improve the quality of education for minority students by transporting them to so-called better schools located outside their neighborhoods.

By 1968, antibusing sentiment had reached critical mass, and police presence was required to escort buses carrying black students to and from several Boston area high schools under a hail of rocks and bottles, accompanied by the chants of angry whites clutching signs that read "Die, niggers" and "Bus the niggers back to Africa." Race relations in Boston were always volatile, but forced busing caused the city to explode.

Living under these circumstances made it nearly impossible for blacks to escape the horror of a cruel past. This past, fraught with a shamefully evil history of involuntary servitude—which sprang from the label of inhumanity that had been forced upon blacks—served as an indelible reminder that they were defenseless victims of an oppressive mind-set that, on a daily basis, still relentlessly reared its ugly head. African Americans found themselves not only disenfranchised, but, even after having been granted legal citizenship under the Fourteenth Amendment to the United States Constitution, also still blatantly denied access to the fundamental freedoms to which they were entitled. The preamble to the Declaration of Independence clearly states, in part:

We hold these truths to be self-evident, that all men are created equal, that they are endowed by their Creator with certain unalienable Rights, that among these are Life, Liberty and the pursuit of Happiness.

Despite the moral sanctity of these words, black people still couldn't go to a park, the store, or beyond the boundaries of their own neighborhood without being taunted, chased, and attacked by those who considered them to be inferior, or even less than human.

On April 4, 1968, Dr. Martin Luther King Jr. was assassinated as he stood on the balcony of the Lorraine Motel in Memphis, Tennessee. He had traveled to Memphis to show his support for a nonviolent boycott by black sanitation workers attempting to address labor issues related to job safety, equal wages and benefits, and union recognition.

The night before he was assassinated, Dr. King delivered an impassioned speech, "I've Been to the Mountaintop," during which he seemed to harbor no fear of his own mortality; somehow, he knew his destiny was about to take an alternate path. With clear conviction, he acknowledged the fact that he might not get to the "Promised Land" with those for whom he was willing to give his life. That revelation, however, did not stop him from imploring his followers to continue the nonviolent struggle with the same unwavering faith and determination he espoused.

The very next day, he was gone.

Dr. King's death was the spark that ignited the powder keg, and African Americans across the country took to the streets to demand justice in any way they could. There was a collective sense of hopelessness among them, and this shocking reality made many feel they were faced with two diametrically opposing options from which to choose: the slow-moving, inequitable wheels of justice to which black people were historically subjected, or taking matters into their own hands through civil disobedience and race riots.

Many chose to employ the latter.

In the days that followed Dr. King's assassination, buildings were set ablaze and cars were torched, mobs of angry people attacked each other, and stores were looted. President Johnson mobilized the National Guard and deployed them to cities around the country in an attempt to quell the violence, but the initial response to this action was one of defiance that only served to escalate the unrest.

James Brown, the Godfather of Soul, was scheduled to

perform at a concert in Boston on the evening following Dr. King's assassination, and it was reported that heated discussions were held among city officials to determine whether the concert should be cancelled. Kevin White, the mayor of Boston at the time, attempted to keep the cauldron from boiling over by asking a local television station to broadcast the concert live. This arrangement made it possible for fans to stay at home and watch the concert on television.

James Brown did, in fact, perform that night, and he seized the opportunity to speak not only to black people in Boston, but also to the larger African American community across the country. He urged them to keep their cool and show restraint by not acting out in a violent manner, despite the incendiary circumstances that gripped the nation. Black Bostonians—faced with fear, apprehension, and the prospect of an uncertain future—listened to his appeal, and, for the most part, responded by *not* burning the city to the ground.

Two months later, on June 8, 1968, Robert F. Kennedy, brother of the slain president, was assassinated at the Embassy Hotel in Los Angeles, California, while campaigning for the Democratic Party's nomination for president of the United States. The Kennedys were a powerful and politically entrenched family, and, during President Kennedy's administration, he and his brother Robert—the U.S. attorney general at the time—found themselves embroiled in the issue of segregation in the south.

The gravity of the Freedom Riders incident had prompted government intervention, and, as a result, martial law was declared in the state of Alabama. This declaration placed the

Kennedy brothers at the center of the civil rights movement, and, by default, they assumed the role of being advocates of equal rights for minorities.

At the same time, however, the administration had the task not only of addressing the scourges of poverty in America—where the downtrodden were seeking to achieve a better way of life for themselves and their families—but also of facing the need to diffuse the threat of the Cold War and nuclear proliferation that had led to the Cuban missile crisis.

When Bobby Kennedy died, so too did the empathetic bond he had with those who were less fortunate, and African Americans mourned as if a member of their own extended family had been killed. What's more, it left many of them with the stark realization that yet another individual committed to making the world a better place had now been silenced.

The American baby boomer generation played a pivotal role during these times by becoming a vital force that advocated for a more tolerant and loving world, even as governments across the globe focused on self-serving interests that tested each other's strength and resolve through political manipulation and military conflict.

Woodstock, originally billed as a two-day arts and music fair, turned into a huge lovefest during which over a half million flower children descended upon Bethel, a small town in upstate New York, in August of 1969. For three straight days, twenty-four hours a day, a live concert of nonstop music was played by some of the world's most famous, as well as up-and-coming, artists. This event gave voice to a cultural movement that sought to end the war and achieve world peace.

As the unrest in America continued, and incidents of deadly violence crystallized opposing viewpoints, race relations across the country further eroded. The thought of a black family going to Martha's Vineyard (or anywhere else, for that matter) caused concern. Would it be wise to leave the safety and security of our small black community in West Medford? Would we be singled out, beaten up, or possibly killed by gangs of angry Caucasians, who, because of indifference or ignorance, did not understand our plight? These questions haunted us as our mother contemplated whether we should travel to the Vineyard.

We decided to go, and what we encountered when we arrived was the polar opposite of what we expected to find, given the destructive path the country was on at that time.

Instead of being greeted by hatred and aggression, we found an island community that appeared to be somewhat detached from what the rest of America was experiencing.

This is not to suggest that racism did not exist there; it most certainly did. Black people were victims of institutionalized racism and prejudice on Martha's Vineyard, just as they were everywhere else. They had no access to jobs other than those that were menial in nature, so they were cooks, butlers, drivers, servants, nannies, dishwashers, landscapers, and laborers. The opportunity to purchase or run a business was all but unheard of, and the ability to acquire real estate—with the exception of in very specific areas in Oak Bluffs—eluded them.

It is a documented fact that black people, at one time, were not allowed to stay at any of the white-owned hotels, cottages, or guesthouses on the Vineyard; nor were they welcomed to become members of the island's golf, yacht, beach, or boating clubs. African Americans were never seen on the grounds of these establishments, except on rare occasions when they had to perform a task deemed to be too lowly or inappropriate for white people.

Although it is true that these societal ills have always existed on the Vineyard, I was fortunate to have been there at a time when it wasn't as obvious—it was more covert—compared to the reckless bouts of denigration we had to endure on a daily basis back in Boston.

In Oak Bluffs, the mainstream view of a society preoccupied with who you were, where you came from, or the color of your skin, did not seem to matter that much—at least for my generation. Whether you were black or white, Indian or Portuguese, Jewish or Cape Verdean, or any other race or combination thereof, it was not emphasized; in Oak Bluffs, most people looked upon you as a human being, first and foremost, and refrained from engaging in stereotyping, categorizing, or labeling.

At no time throughout the decades of summers I spent on the Vineyard did I ever hear anyone openly call me a "nigger," "spook," "coon," "monkey," "jungle bunny," "Sambo," "shine," or any of the other derogatory epithets routinely spewed with hatred toward people of African descent elsewhere. It was almost as if parts of the island existed on a higher plane than the rest of the country, making the expression of "Come one, come all" seem more realistic. Oak Bluffs exuded a feeling of acceptance and inclusiveness unique to the place, a quality all but devoid everywhere else.

The Vineyard We Knew

The Vineyard, back then, was one of the first places in which I witnessed interracial couples come out of the shadows and walk freely down the street together without having to worry about being gawked at, ridiculed, or rejected. There was an understanding that respect was something that was earned and reciprocated, and the expression of one's individuality was not only encouraged, but considered to be a rite of passage. It was a place that celebrated the diverse qualities each of us possessed— where there was a seat for you at the table, regardless of your ideology or beliefs.

Perhaps these are just a few of the many reasons why tens of thousands of visitors continue to come to Martha's Vineyard each year. A common belief shared among those touched by the Vineyard experience is that, once you set foot on the island, all your cares will inexplicably melt away.

Whether you happened to be there for a day, a week, a month, or the entire summer was immaterial; it was a place where you were not only able to let your hair down, but also your guard. It was a "summer place" unlike any other.

Walter Norris, Kevin, and Chuck at South Beach

Chapter 16

South Beach

*O*f all the wonderful beaches that grace the shores of Martha's Vineyard, one has attributes unlike any of the others. South Beach, on a section of the island known as Katama and part of the town of Edgartown, faces the more turbulent waters of the south shore. Covering a distance of over three miles, it easily qualifies as being one of the most expansive beaches on the Vineyard, and, as such, provides ample room for those seeking recreation by the sea.

This long strip of shoreline—composed of finely textured sand that creates dunes of various configurations—appears to go on forever and was (back then, at least) unobstructed by any sign of development. Beach grass, securely anchored in the sand, is whipped into frenzy by the relentless southeast winds blowing off the ocean. Back and forth, up and down, the tall, slender blades bow in deference to nature's powerful breath.

Walls of ocean water pound against the shore and retreat back into the depths, as wave after wave, rising high from the ocean's surface, roll onto the beach in succession, depositing tons of sand, seashells, stones, seaweed, and anything else caught in the clutches of the Atlantic's ferocious currents.

South Beach attracts a wide range of visitors, from skilled surfers seeking the thrill of riding the powerful waves, to casual swimmers, to those who want nothing more than to stand at the water's edge and play tag with the crashing surf as it tumbles onto the warm sand.

But it is as dangerous as it is beautiful. Whirlpools and riptides are common, and diligence is required to ensure a safe experience as you playfully romp in the untamed waters along this beach.

The vastness of South Beach accommodates an array of activities, particularly as the island has become more populated with summer tourists. Individuals and entire families stretch out on blankets or under beach umbrellas for a day of swimming and sunbathing amid the breathtaking sights of this beautiful seaside habitat.

Some of the more popular activities at the beach include volleyball, badminton, Frisbee tossing, kite flying, football or baseball throwing, and barbequing. Fishermen sit in beach chairs at the water's edge with their rods propped up, awaiting the tug of an award-winning striped bass. At the end of the day, as the sun sinks below the western horizon, taking along its reddish orange hue, the flicker of a campfire in the distance becomes brighter as it is carefully stoked in a shallow pit dug into the sand along the beach.

Our trips to South Beach occurred long before it was discovered by the masses. Back then, we parked the car anywhere we desired along the desolate two-lane road, then took one of the sandy paths and walked for miles over the dunes. Often, when we scanned the entire area, we found we were the only ones there—except for the ocean, sand, sun, and seagulls. Audible sounds were limited to the splashing of the waves, the howl of the wind, and an occasional cry from an osprey, hawk, or seagull as it soared high above in the infinitely spacious sky.

I was pedaling my bike up the steep hill on School Street one hot summer afternoon, heading for home, when I noticed my brother standing at the top of the street, watching me as I approached.

"Kevin, where have you been? We've been looking all over for you."

"I was just riding around. Why?"

"We're going to the beach."

"Which one?"

"South Beach," he said.

"South Beach? How are we getting there?"

"Mr. Norris is taking us. You'd better get to the house and get ready because we'll be leaving soon."

I took a shortcut through the schoolyard and made my way to the house, where I found Nana standing in the yard, talking with Mr. Norris.

"Hi, Nana. Hello, Mr. Norris," I said.

"Didn't you hear me calling you?" she asked.

"No, Nana. I was riding around on my bike."

"Go put your bathing suit on; we'll be leaving for the beach in a few minutes."

The Vineyard We Knew

"Yes, Nana."

Before long, we were on our way to South Beach, and once again found ourselves tightly packed into the back of Mr. Norris's car. Cruising southeast from Oak Bluffs, we traveled through the outskirts of Edgartown to Katama, where a sparsely populated landscape of farms and fields led to the open ocean. We motored past bales of hay that looked like giant spools of shredded wheat cereal neatly stacked in a field just off the road. A thin, wire fence surrounded this field, and the flat terrain stretched out as far as the eye could see, making us feel as if we were lost in time on an old farm in Kansas.

A weathered silo stood at attention—a lonely soldier—as the wind gently blew through cornstalks, causing them to sway as if they were inverted pendulums. On the opposite side of the road, an old red tractor sat motionless between rows of vegetables reaching upward from the fertile Vineyard soil.

When we arrived at South Beach, Mr. Norris pulled the car onto an embankment in front of a large sand dune that blocked the view of the ocean. When I got out of the car, the hot pavement began to heat up the rubber on the bottom of my sneakers, so I ran down a narrow path to the beach. I removed my sneakers and socks, freeing my feet from bondage, then sank them into the warm, soothing sand as I ran to the water's edge. While stopping for a moment to catch my breath, I heard my cousin Vincent yell, "Hey, Kevin, wait up!"

Behind me, I saw my brother, sister, and cousins, as well as Nana and Mr. Norris, walking over a dune and down the path. They caught up with me, and, when we all reached the edge of the shore, huge waves rolled onto the beach, just as we had

Spools of hay on a farm

come to expect. There wasn't another soul around for miles; it felt as if we had the entire island to ourselves.

"The water looks too rough to go swimming today," Nana said.

"You're right, Carrie. The rip currents are very strong. Let's hike down the beach instead and see what we can find," Mr. Norris said.

We kids—disappointed that we couldn't go swimming— started walking barefoot along the shore and entertained ourselves by dodging the foam left behind by hissing waves sliding back into the ocean.

I turned my attention out to sea, to where the sky met the water, and was temporarily mesmerized by the sight of an oil tanker many miles away. It appeared to be no larger than the head of a pin, and slowly inched across the horizon before finally slipping out of sight. The tranquility of the moment was interrupted by the voice of my cousin Charlene.

"Hey, let's look for some seashells," she said.

In an instant, Charlene, Joanne, and Carmella ran ahead to scour the sand for any shells that might be worth collecting. I was content with searching for flat rocks to skip on the surface of the choppy water. Chuck and Vincent took off over a sand dune and ran through the tall beach grass, briefly disappearing from sight until Nana's call yanked them back like a yo-yo on the end of a string.

Fifteen minutes later, the girls returned with a variety of colorful shells—sand dollar, scallop, quahog, snail, crab, clam, mussel—and even a few live starfish.

"We'll be able to make a lot of necklaces with these shells," Charlene said.

"We sure will," Joanne and Carmella agreed.

As we strolled along the beach for about a quarter mile, we saw a flock of seagulls hovering in the distance, diving down on to something lying on the sand at the water's edge.

"Let's go check it out," Mr. Norris said.

We trotted to where all the commotion was. There, sprawled both on the beach and partly submerged in the water, was the carcass of a semidecomposed sand shark.

"So, this is the reason for the seagulls' feeding frenzy," Vincent said.

"What do you think happened to this shark?" I asked.

"It could have gotten sick or been involved in a fight with another shark and got washed ashore," Mr. Norris answered.

"Look at the gashes in its side," Nana said.

"Maybe it got hit by a boat," Chuck said.

"That could be, Chuck," Mr. Norris replied.

The stench of decomposition made us back away from the fish, and, as soon we did, the seagulls resumed fighting among themselves for another chance to peck at it. Without warning, the wind picked up, prompting Mr. Norris to look out over the water.

"The sky is beginning to look threatening; let's turn around and head back to the car," he said. The eight of us did an about-face and started back.

Almost immediately, the sun disappeared behind a bank of dark nimbus clouds, and a strong gust of wind kicked up the sand, blowing it into our faces and relentlessly stinging us as tiny particles of sand hit our bare skin. We were forced to stop and cover our eyes to protect ourselves and help us see.

What had started out as a leisurely stroll along the shore

suddenly became a punishing journey as each step pitted us against the prevailing head winds, and the rumble of thunder shook the ground beneath us.

Fortunately, we made it back to the car just as the heavens opened up, unleashing a deluge followed closely by a clap of lightning.

Once safely back in the car, Mr. Norris started her up and whisked us away from the inclement weather that had engulfed beautiful South Beach. Soon after making our escape, before we even arrived back at the house, the sun timidly peeked through the clouds. The storm had chugged away just as quickly as it had appeared.

Such was the case with thunderstorms on the Vineyard. Sometimes they had tropical characteristics, but, at other times, they lasted for days—making for a long and soggy stay in our grandmother's house—where, under those conditions, mildew was king.

The Jetties

Chapter 17

The Jetties

*S*tanding guard at the entrance to the Oak Bluffs harbor were the jetties—two man-made configurations of boulders piled on top of one another, reaching into the cold Atlantic like old, weathered fingers. The gateway to the harbor, these mammoth stones were the destination of countless seafaring vessels and crew; if reached, they offered the promise of safety from the indiscriminate dangers lurking at sea.

Anchored to the outermost boulder of one of the jetties was a metal structure that housed a flashing red light which, for decades, guided boats safely into the harbor. A continuous parade of traffic entered and exited through the narrow waterway between the rocks.

The jetties sat on the northeast face of the island, just beyond the center of town. Easily accessible, they were a favorite place for my friends and I to hang out.

The rocks on the jetties were of various shapes and sizes; some had jagged edges, while others were round and smooth to

the touch. This solid barrier provided us with a fun, but dangerous, form of recreation.

We used to scale the stones boldly, then run out to the very
end as fast as we could, jumping from one boulder to another
while carefully planting our feet on the hard surfaces. During
high tide, many of the rocks were submerged, so we had to alter
our path to compensate for those no longer accessible. It was
always a challenge not to slip on the sand and seaweed exposed
at low tide, or fall and scrape our knees on the sharp barnacles
attached to the rocks below. We especially had to be wary of
falling into the water, which we took great care to avoid at all
costs. We also had to refrain from accidentally bumping into
people fishing from or walking on the jetties.

On hot summer days, my friends and I spent entire afternoons diving off a particular rock about three-quarters of the
way out. Long and flat, it jutted out over the water, making it
perfect for leaping into the cool, refreshing ocean.

Nestled between the jetties and the Oak Bluffs Wharf was
Town Beach; the locals used to call it Jetty Beach. This narrow
strip of coarse white sand, small rocks, and seashells was a popular place for islanders and tourists to enjoy picturesque views of
Cape Cod and Nantucket Sound. People swam, fished, sun-
bathed, and sat on beach chairs or blankets, their coolers within
reach. I went to that beach often, long before I knew how to
swim, for some of my friends habitually hung out there or at the
jetties on most days.

At the back of the beach was a six-foot-high cement seawall that not only protected the street above, but also served
as a walkway between the wharf and the jetties. Wooden

wave-breakers—strategically positioned on the sand at perpendicular angles to the shoreline—met the gentle surf as it folded onto the beach.

The ocean on this side of the jetties was great for swimming because the depth gradually increased as you waded in, unlike at other beaches, where a sudden drop could have you over your head after only a few steps. The water was clear and calm, with a sandy bottom, allowing us easily to see lobsters and crabs scurrying about the submerged rocks. Horseshoe crabs—appropriately named for their round, armorlike shells that resembled the shape of a horseshoe—were in abundance at this beach and often startled us as they darted across the ocean floor beneath the surface of the shallow water.

A private beach club on the opposite side of the jetties touted a well-groomed bathing area for affluent white tourists. Complete with bathhouses and finely sifted sand, this establishment provided members a level of service and amenities that didn't exist for the rest of us. This particular beach club went to great lengths to accentuate the striking differences between the "haves" and the "have-nots," offering luxuries that working-class people were not only unfamiliar with, but were allowed to observe only from afar.

Waiters and waitresses shuttled refreshments to people either stretched out on cots or sitting under beach umbrellas woven from the finest hand-stitched cloth. They had access to soft, absorbent beach towels that seemed to appear magically after a nod or a simple gesture.

Not that any of us were attempting to emulate the privileges of those people on the other side of the jetties, but we had our own version of a bathhouse on our side, too—the public restroom next to the Steamship Authority wharf—where a steady stream of people lined up to use the soiled facilities. For some odd reason, the radiators were always turned on full blast and it was stifling hot inside, regardless of the fact that it was the height of the summer season. In an attempt to air the place out, the windows were left open to allow heat and the acidic odor of urine to escape.

My friends and I were often amused by the reactions of those at the beach club when someone swam across the channel into their so-called *exclusive* area. Expressions of dismay were etched on faces red as lobsters from too much sun, and it wasn't unreasonable to imagine people in the clubhouse with their hands tightly gripping telephones, ready to summon the harbor master, local police, or even the Coast Guard to intercept any intruder with the audacity to invade their space.

Although this refusal by common folk to conform to their place in society was routinely viewed as offensive by the privileged members of this club, these two opposing lifestyles—depicting the stark differences inherent in race and class—were able to coexist peacefully without any major altercations.

Because we were teenagers, at times we did silly things that the slightest attention to common sense might have averted. One such incident almost cost me my life. As mentioned, I used to run the entire length of the jetties with my friends long before I knew how to swim.

On a warm, sunny afternoon without a cloud in the sky, I

was standing about midway out on the jetties, watching people fishing. The calm, hypnotizing effect of the wake from boats entering and leaving the harbor lulled me into a trance. Scattered about the rocks were fishing rods, tackle boxes, and bait composed of squid and sea worms; the odor of freshly caught fish was in the air. It was unusually crowded on the jetties that day, and there was barely enough room to maneuver around all the people.

While facing the harbor entrance, I felt a powerful lunge into my back and was instantly catapulted into the deep side of the channel. As I hit the water, I panicked and sank below the surface. After bobbing back up, I could barely hear the shouts of several people on the jetties because the sound of their voices became garbled as my ears quickly filled with water. Desperately attempting to feel for the bottom with my feet, I realized the channel was much too deep; the ocean floor was far beyond my reach.

Consequently, I sank like a stone. My violent thrashing about was an exercise in futility; it just made me sink deeper and faster. A sharp burning sensation filled my lungs as I gasped and choked on the salty ocean water. Never before having been in water over my head, I could not fathom how to save myself from this impending doom.

But, when I went under for the third time, a gentle calm swept over me—a warm and soothing kind of comfort. At that moment, my fear and terror all but vanished; somehow I knew I would be okay. Without realizing it, I began to paddle my arms and kick my feet and slowly inched myself closer to the jetties until I felt one of the huge rocks below me. Exhausted and scared, I crawled out of the channel and onto a boulder with the help of some nearby onlookers.

Because of that incident, I went to the beach every day until I learned how to swim. After several weeks of practice, I gradually lost my fear of the ocean as I became more familiar with the mechanics of floating, treading water, and the relationship between mind and body that facilitated the act of swimming. Never again did I want to experience the horrific feeling of almost drowning.

Who pushed me into the channel that day remains a mystery, but I guess it was one of my mischievous friends playing a near-fatal prank on me.

The steamship *Nobska*

Chapter 18

Coin Diving

*T*he summers I spent on the Vineyard allowed me not only to develop close relationships with kids born and raised there, but also to learn from them some of life's most valuable lessons. My Vineyard friends were true "islanders" in every sense of the word, and they personified that in ways I could only imagine.

Their stock was from generations of families who had lived, worked, retired, and died on this small piece of utopia. These earthy people passed down a legacy that embodied integrity and pride in who they were and what they stood for, all evidenced by their quality of life. A common characteristic among those who lived on Martha's Vineyard was that they believed in old-fashioned values. Among them, your word was your bond, and all it took to consummate a deal was a simple handshake.

I was fortunate to have learned a great skill during my fourteenth summer on the island when I was introduced to a little-known cottage industry by a friend of mine, Ritchie. "Coin diving," as it was called, was the perfect antidote to a Vineyard teenager's dilemma of wanting to earn some money while not being old enough to work. Imagine, having cash literally thrown at you for the sake of entertaining tourists arriving at Oak Bluffs or waiting aboard the ferry to continue their journey to Nantucket.

Every morning at approximately 10:35—rain or shine—I listened for the raspy, hollow-sounding whistle of the steamship *Nobska*, announcing its arrival at the wharf in Oak Bluffs. Scheduled to dock at 10:45, it was the first of three daily boats we coin-dived from, the other two arriving at 4:15 and 7:45. In a manner that emulated a form of classic behavioral conditioning, that whistle was my cue to hop on my gold, three-speed bicycle and pedal as fast as I could—my swimming trunks on and goggles and flippers securely fastened to the handlebars— for the seven-minute ride into town to meet the boat.

As I rode my bike up the grassy slope of my grandmother's driveway and on to Pacific Avenue, the rear tire skidded on the sand and propelled me down the street in a flash. With increasing speed, I winged my way toward my destination and noticed, only by way of peripheral vision, familiar neighborhood sights as they whisked by as if they were still images strung together on a reel of film.

As I continued to ride, my breathing got deeper, and I felt my pulse rising with each successive rotation of the pedals. A cool breeze bounced off my face, evaporating the beads of sweat beginning to stream down my forehead. Turning on to New York Avenue, maximum speed was reached as the force of gravity pulled the bike down the hill past Sunset Lake and the harbor.

Coin Diving

From that point, the wharf was less than one minute away, just beyond the Flying Horses and Ocean Park.

My arrival at Oak Bluffs Wharf found me in the midst of the usual cast of characters, anywhere from six to ten teenagers, all waiting for the steamship *Nobska* to make its scheduled stop at the Vineyard before continuing on to Nantucket Island. I leaned my bike against a metal fence that served as a barrier between the sidewalk above and the steep incline leading to the water's edge below. While securing the bike to the fence with a click of the combination lock, I turned to see where the boat was and saw my friend Ritchie walking toward me.

"I was wondering where you were," he said, as we high-fived each other.

"I was a little behind the eight ball this morning, but I made it," I said.

"Glad you did," he replied.

"Now come on man, you *know* I wouldn't miss this for the world!"

"Yeah, I know. Besides, we need you out there to help deal with the other divers," he said.

Ritchie was not only an islander; he was an energetic, young entrepreneur well versed in all aspects of coin diving, particularly when it came to maximizing profits by eliminating the competition.

Our miniature enterprise was made up of four friends— Ritchie, Tim, Mike, and me—who, at one time, had been fierce competitors, until we decided to join forces and divide the money we collected from each boat. It was a wise business decision and one that proved to be quite lucrative for a group of boys between the ages of twelve and fourteen.

The Vineyard We Knew

Through the application of a business concept known as "economies of scale," we were able to corner the coin diving market and make the most money, hands down.

And how did we do this? Let me explain.

Each member of the team was responsible for executing a particular assignment while in the water. One of us acted as the decoy, which involved staking out an area next to the boat and urging spectators—either waiting on the boat or walking along the boardwalk—to toss us nickels, dimes, quarters, half-dollars, or silver dollars. On several occasions, a more generous spectator tightly folded up a one-dollar or five-dollar bill and threw it down to us. We had no interest in collecting pennies, allowing them to float to the ocean floor for the other coin divers to retrieve.

The repetitive chant—"How 'bout a coin?"—echoed off the side of the boat, inducing tourists to dig into their pockets for some coined currency in response to our unique form of panhandling.

As soon as the coins began to fly, one of us ran interference by distracting the other coin divers, preventing them from swimming after the coins. This was accomplished by bumping them away from the area where the coins were tossed, pulling their goggles or fins off, or grabbing on to their arms, legs, or feet, rendering them immobile.

The two of us that remained caught the coins before they floated to the bottom. We then stored them in our cheeks until we all swam back to shore.

Coin Diving

Looking out beyond the wharf, we saw the arriving steamship list slightly to the left as she made a hard right turn toward the dock. It was time for us to go to work.

Thick, black smoke billowed from the slender metal smoke-stack on the upper deck of the *Nobska* and drifted up into the bright morning sky, obscuring the view of the horizon in the distance.

"Let's make some money!" Ritchie yelled, in a manner similar to what a military general might say to motivate his troops.

"It looks like a full boat this morning!" I said, with excitement.

"Yeah, but we have some stiff competition today," Tim replied.

And he was correct; we had six other rogue coin divers to contend with.

"No problem. Let's just do what we always do and we'll be fine," I said, with a confident smirk.

The four of us waded into the water a few feet from the rocky shore, and, after securing our goggles to our faces and fins on our feet, we dove into the cold ocean next to the wharf. The tide was high and the current was strong, which required us to expend more energy than usual to swim out to the boat and maintain position once we were out there.

The depth where the boat docked varied on any given day because the tides were in control, but it could easily be twenty-five to thirty-feet deep. My friends and I had honed the skill of snatching falling coins from the water before they reached the ocean floor, regardless of how deep the water happened to be. Otherwise, we would have to dive to the bottom to retrieve them, an act that required a strong set of lungs and good muscle strength to keep from being swept away by the raging currents below.

Another hazard to be aware of was the propellers underneath the vessel which, if we were not careful, could suck us under the water as the steamship left the dock.

Each time I swam out to meet the boat, I glanced at the wooden pilings supporting the wharf and noticed the sharp barnacles attached to them as they rose from the dark depths. It was not uncommon to encounter a variety of marine life while out there in the mysterious ocean. I saw sharks, manta rays, Portuguese man-of-war jellyfish, crabs, lobsters, many types of fish, and all kinds of aquatic plants, including seaweed and ocean grass that gently swayed back and forth beneath the ocean's surface.

I was afraid when I made my first attempt at coin diving because it didn't take much of an imagination to conjure up scenarios that would lead to my demise. It was fortunate that my experiences occurred before the movie *Jaws* was filmed on the island. Otherwise, I probably would never even have considered coin diving.

When we reached the boat, we found it was indeed packed with tourists. After joining the other coin divers, we began repeating the chant, "How 'bout a coin?" Almost immediately, the first coin was thrown and we sprang into action.

Tim, as the decoy, cordoned off the area where the coin had been tossed by splashing and bumping several of our competitors out of the way. Ritchie detained the rest of them by grabbing their legs. Mike and I were responsible for going after the coins, and I dove down to retrieve this first one, a Kennedy half-dollar. This activity continued as coin after coin was tossed in succession. By the time the boat left the dock fifteen minutes later, our cheeks were bulging with silver coins.

Our team swam back to shore and met on the sidewalk next to the ticket office to divvy up the take. On any lucrative boat, we averaged about five dollars each, more than enough to fund our individual wants. That might include purchasing food, candy, soda (or cigarettes for those who smoked), playing pinball, pitching coins against the curbstone—whatever we chose to do to pass the time between boats.

My daily routine included jaunts across the street to the Captain's Table, a small greasy-spoon diner that resembled a railroad car, where breakfast, lunch, or dinner was available any time of the day. It reminded me of the old, sleazy diners you saw in detective movies, usually situated in a seedy part of town, and in which, more often than not, the action took place on a dark, cold, and rainy night. These diners typically had a complement of regulars satisfying their needs for a cheap meal.

At the Captain's Table, however, the action was the exchange of tall tales among those who frequented the diner, and the place reeked of cigarette smoke and cooking grease. Tiny booths hugged the outer wall, and a row of metal stools—with rotating red seat cushions—lined the entire length of the counter. I ordered a slice of Boston cream pie and a large Coke each time I went there, but the sugar high I got from ingesting that unhealthy combination of junk food—and the crash that always followed—made me wonder whether it was worth my hard-earned cash.

After leaving the diner, I headed back to the wharf to find a spirited game of pitching coins taking place. The object was simple. Standing behind a makeshift line on the street, about ten feet from the sidewalk, players tossed coins in an attempt to get theirs closest to the curb. The one whose coin ended up being the closest collected all the coins tossed from that round. If you happened to be skilled enough to get your coin to lean against the curb, there was no question as to the winner, and any attempts by other players to dispute the results were thwarted.

I elected not to participate in this activity because I had other places I wanted to spend my hard-earned money. Instead, I left my friends and went to play a couple of games of pinball at the Flying Horses, where a dime would buy a single game and a quarter would be good for three plays. I was by no means a pinball wizard, but I held my own by occasionally beating the high score for a replay, or I'd win another game by matching the last two digits of my score with a random, machine-generated number.

When I had had enough of manhandling the pinball machines to the point of tilting a few games, I briefly stopped at the novelty shop in a wooden building next to the Flying Horses. You couldn't miss it because it was painted a hideous canary yellow. This place was home to every kind of trinket, souvenir, and penny candy imaginable, and easily lured both young and old alike into its grasp.

The proprietor of this establishment was an old, gentle, heavyset woman with stringy gray hair and eyeglasses who always had a friendly word for anyone who happened to come in. Because of my overactive sweet tooth, and fondness at the time for Mounds and Almond Joy candy bars, I never failed to plunk down my ten cents to buy one or the other. Each time I did this, the old woman would ask, "Is your name Peter or Paul?"

I simply smiled, took my candy bar, and went on my way, thinking she was confusing me for someone else.

Now this routine went on for weeks. When I finally grew tired of repeatedly being queried, I got up the nerve to say something in response to her constant inquiries. When she asked again, "Is your name Peter or Paul?" I responded by saying, "Neither. Why do you ask?"

"I ask because you come in here every day—without fail—and buy either a Mounds or Almond Joy candy bar."

"That's right; I do," I said.

"Did you know they are made by a company called Peter Paul?"

It finally occurred to me, she had been joking with me all along.

"No, I didn't. And, besides, my name isn't Peter or Paul; it's Kevin," I said.

She must have found my reaction amusing because she belted out a hearty laugh—overshadowed by the sound of the *Nobska's* whistle. I knew I had to get back to the wharf immediately to make the afternoon boat for coin diving.

"I've got to get going; I don't want to miss the boat!" I said.

"Okay. Good luck, and don't forget your candy bar," she replied.

"Thanks!" I said.

I grabbed the Almond Joy off the counter and made it back to the wharf just in time to swim out to where my friends were waiting for the first coins to be thrown.

The afternoon and early evening boats carrying tourists back to the mainland were never as lucrative as the ones going to the islands. Perhaps it was because the passengers on board were simply exhausted and broke from vacationing; they just wanted to get home. But that reality never discouraged us from swimming out to the boat and asking for a coin anyway.

The last ferry of the day was the *Nantucket*, which arrived at 7:45 from the island of Nantucket before continuing on to Woods Hole. She docked at the outer slip at the far end of the wharf—in *very* deep water.

This was the time of day when the sun was rapidly setting, and visibility was limited to about seven to ten feet below the surface. Consequently, when a coin was tossed under those conditions, you had as few as five seconds to retrieve it before it disappeared into an abyss of murky darkness. This made even the most experienced coin diver approach the 7:45 ferry with both respect and trepidation.

On the positive side, this challenge encouraged our group to fine-tune its coin diving skills, and, as a result, we were the best coin divers around—hands down.

Sunset Lake

Chapter 19

Sunset Lake

*L*ess than a quarter of a mile from my grandmother's house was a small body of water called Sunset Lake. It sat across the street from the Oak Bluffs harbor and was bordered by New York Avenue on the east, Dukes County Avenue on the south, and Greenleaf Avenue on the west. Calm water and shallow depth made it a natural habitat for a variety of fish, waterfowl, and amphibians that frolicked among the lily pads and other aquatic plant life that flourished there. Several weeping willows grew along the bank of the lake, lazily hanging over the water's edge while providing wildlife a place to hide from predators.

We often walked down to the lake to search for frogs or turtles, or to catch tiny sunfish with crude fishing poles we made by tying a safety pin to a piece of string and wrapping the string around the end of a tree branch. If all else failed, we could always just watch people navigate the paddleboats available to rent for a small fee.

The Vineyard We Knew

One day, Chuck and Carmella went across the street to the harbor to watch fishermen unload their boats and clean their catch right there on the dock. Carmella took it upon herself to ask for a few fish heads the fishermen were going to throw away. She and Chuck returned to the lake and tied a piece of rope they had taken from Nana's house around a fish head, tossed it into the water, and dragged it along the bottom close to shore. In no time, the crabs scurried after the fish heads, and Chuck and Carmella immediately scooped them into a net and took them home.

I ambled down to Sunset Lake by myself one afternoon and caught a large snapping turtle with a dark, green shell and vivid yellow and orange markings. I gave it to my sister, Deirdre, and we took this aggressive reptile back to Medford and kept it as a pet over the winter. It didn't take long for us to realize we never should have removed it from its natural habitat. The following spring, we brought it back to Woods Hole—barely still alive— and set it free by tossing it into the ocean next to the Steamship Authority dock. It quickly swam away and disappeared into the dark depths.

The serenity of Sunset Lake gave it an identity unto itself, despite the fact that it was close to downtown where much of the tourism-related activity in Oak Bluffs occurred. The rumble of cars, trucks, and buses passing by the lake never seemed to disrupt the quiet those few steps away. Once there, you felt as if you had walked through an invisible door to another dimension of reality where, visually, everything appeared to be unchanged, but the background noises mysteriously faded away, to be replaced by the soothing sounds of nature.

This tranquil body of water supported a delicate ecosystem

of plants and animals. It wasn't unusual to see pairs of white swans slowly drifting across the surface of the lake with their fledglings following closely behind. On the shore, cottontail rabbits hopped in the grass and nibbled on select varieties of vegetation, while green garter snakes slithered over the ground along the bank in a stealthy fashion, searching for small insects to consume.

><

One summer, my brother's best friend, Bruce, arrived on the island on a Friday evening to spend the weekend with us at Nana's house.

Chuck and Bruce had become the best of friends in the third grade. One morning they had both been standing in the school-yard when Bruce happened to notice my brother. He casually walked over and asked if he wanted to be his best friend. Chuck agreed, and, from that moment, they were inseparable. Bruce's personality was energetic and upbeat, and he had a slight wild streak flowing through him; my brother's demeanor was more reserved. These opposite traits balanced each other perfectly— one of the reasons their friendship worked.

Bruce was like a member of the family, and, long before he had ever come to the island, he was well aware of our experiences on the Vineyard. Over the years, he had heard the stories about our summers at grandmother's house (affectionately referred to as "Carrie's Concentration Camp") and how she never hesitated to beat our asses at the drop of a hat. There was no such thing as a "kid guest" in Nana's eyes. If you stayed at her house, you were treated like one of her own grandchildren, which meant you had to eat what was served, and you were just as susceptible to getting whacked with the strap if you acted up. There were no waivers, no passes, and no exceptions—period.

Nana was fond of Bruce, fortunate for him because, during the two days he spent with us, he got to experience firsthand a weekend at Carrie's, an ordeal like going through military boot camp on Alcatraz Island. True to form, Nana went about her business of running the household and keeping us all in line.

"Wash your face and hands, eat your food, clean up the kitchen, don't stray too far from the house, and be back in when the streetlights come on," Nana barked out like a drill sergeant.

Before dinner, we were all congregating in the small kitchen where Nana was at the stove preparing our meal. Chuck was wearing one of his favorite knit shirts when he and Nana got into a scuffle about an incident in the past. Our grandmother acted as if it had just taken place. In a fit of anger, Nana lunged at my brother, and, in doing so, stained his shirt with the greasy fork in her hand. Chuck, who was very meticulous about his attire, looked at Nana with his mouth hanging open and asked, "Are you out of your mind? You spilled grease on my knit shirt!"

"Who do you think you're talking to?" she snapped.

At that point, I didn't know whether to jump between them or head for the hills. Luckily, they stopped their bickering and avoided an ugly confrontation. As calmer heads prevailed, things quickly returned to normal. This wasn't saying much because one's perception of what is "normal" is relative.

After eating a simple dinner of kidney beans and rice, we kids spent the rest of the evening hanging out on the front porch until it was time to go to bed. Although the porch was screened in, mosquitoes always found a way through the makeshift repairs and taped-up holes—dive-bombing us in waves like Kamikazes in search of a blood meal. The constant, annoying buzzing of mosquitoes hovering around our heads had us smacking ourselves more often than the Three Stooges as we tried our best to kill the swarms of flying, needle-nosed pests. It got to a point where the assault was too overwhelming to endure, and we were forced to run for cover.

Inside, we rubbed calamine lotion on our skin to soothe the fresh bites. Before long, it was time to go to bed and we all claimed our places to sleep for the night.

The following morning, we were milling about the house after breakfast, trying to decide what we were going to do that day.

"Let's take a walk down to Sunset Lake and go on the paddle-boats," Chuck suggested. The rest of us immediately concurred, and, after getting permission to go from Nana, in no time our entourage made its way toward the lake.

We walked through the schoolyard and crossed School Street into an open field, then followed a path to a dirt road along which several small cottages were lined up on one side. Minutes later, we found ourselves at the summit of a grassy hill in Washington Park. Sunset Lake, the harbor, and downtown appeared in the background as if on a picture postcard. In the distance, the tall white cross on top of the Tabernacle majestically rose above the Campground treetops.

The six of us ran down the hill to where the paddleboats were tied to a small, makeshift dock. An attendant sitting under a willow tree at the water's edge got up from his chair as we approached him.

"You kids want to take the paddleboats out?"

"Yes. How much will it cost and for how long?" Chuck asked.

"Fifty cents for fifteen minutes, two people per boat," he answered.

"Okay, we'll take three boats out. That'll be a buck-fifty for the six of us, right?"

"Correct."

After paying the fee, we walked down a wooden plank to the boats and selected the ones we wanted to take out. Chuck and Bruce took one; Charlene and Carmella took another; and Vincent and I hopped into a third.

"How do you work this thing?" I asked.

"All you have to do is pedal like you're on a bicycle and steer with the rudder," the attendant said.

"Okay, let's go!

We began pedaling as instructed, and the three paddleboats slowly eased away from the dock. The attendant carefully watched us from the shore as he yelled out last-minute instructions: "Be sure to stay away from the shoreline, and watch out for the ducks while you're out there!"

Vincent and I navigated our boat to the middle of the lake where Chuck, Bruce, Charlene, and Carmella had already piloted theirs. The water was motionless and reflected like a mirror; the only visible disturbance was symmetrical ripples generated by the wake of the paddleboats as they slowly glided across the lake. There was something therapeutic about being out there on the lake—three boats, six kids, and a flock of mallard ducks bobbing lightly in the water.

After taking the boats around the lake several times, the

novelty of a leisurely sail quickly wore off for Chuck and Bruce, now intent on delving into more challenging pursuits. They broke away from our flotilla and proceeded full speed ahead toward a flock of ducks on the far side of the lake.

My initial thought was that they simply wanted to get a closer look, but, as they drew closer to the ducks, it was clear to me they had no intention of slowing down—or stopping.

"Hey, what are you kids doing? Watch out for those ducks!" the attendant screamed from the shore.

But it was too late. In a stunt that made me think of Captain Bligh in its ruthlessness, they chugged their paddleboat until they overtook several of the helpless birds, resulting in their demise. In addition to hearing panicked sounds of distress, we also looked on in disbelief as a bunch of feathers shot up into the air and gently floated back down to the surface of the water. Fond of animals, I was shocked by the reckless display of carnage Chuck and Bruce had chosen to engage in.

We were ordered to return the boats to the dock immediately. As we did, the attendant launched into a diatribe of threats, ending with him saying he was going to call the police.

That was all we needed to hear. While making our way back to shore, the six of us engaged in a telepathic form of communication, and, without uttering a word, we knew exactly what to do. Just before reaching the dock, we leaped from the paddleboats, hightailed it through the water, and sprinted up the hill toward the house, knowing full well Nana would kick our behinds if she ever found out what had happened.

We shuddered at the thought of a police car pulling up to Nana's house to escort us in handcuffs to the ferry, to be thrown off the island like a bunch of hardened criminals. This fear haunted us for several days afterward, so much so that we went to great lengths to avoid going into town by way of the route that passed the lake. We didn't want to be recognized as the duck killers.

Fortunately, Nana never learned about what happened that day, and our lives returned to normal shortly thereafter.

Several decades later, I shared this story with a friend while relaxing on the front deck of the new home my brother had built. And where did my brother choose to build his new home? Why, he built it overlooking Sunset Lake, of course.

Flying Horses

Chapter 20

Hanging Out

My teenage years on the island were not as challenging as in the earlier times, when my grandmother had shrewdly watched every move and kept me within arm's reach. At seventy-five, however, Nana was beginning to show signs of aging as she approached the winter season of her life.

I now had the freedom to go places and do things I was never allowed to do before—an unaccustomed privilege, to be sure. As always, I had to behave myself while I was out, and I continued to be held to the highest standards of account-ability for my actions. It was impossible to know who was out there waiting to report any act of delinquent behavior back to my grandmother, for her network of friends on the Vineyard reached far and wide. Nana's feistiness was strong in spite of her age, and, whenever she felt it necessary, she had no prob-lem reining me in.

Circuit Avenue—the main road in downtown Oak Bluffs—was a narrow, one-way street at the epicenter of where all the action took place, and, as such, had an eccentric ambience. This busy thoroughfare was on a hill, with angled parking spaces tightly crammed together on the left side. Traffic jams were common; vehicles slowly crept up the street as drivers repeatedly circled the block in search of a place to park. The only time a motorist stopped was to allow pedestrians to cross, or for a car to back out of a space. The narrow sidewalks on either side were inadequate for accommodating the mobs of people wending their ways up and down Circuit Avenue.

Tourists darted in and out of establishments like thousands of ants, and faint music emanated from local bars as you meandered your way through the crowds. The aroma of culinary delights from nearby restaurants stimulated your nose and made your mouth water. That tantalizing sensation was rivaled only by the decadent smell of chocolate fudge and peanut brittle being made at Hilliard's, and the delightful sight of saltwater taffy for sale at Darling's—both stores a confectioner's dream.

Local law enforcement officers acted like part-time police academy recruits-in-training, and, as such, provided their own unique brand of incompetent entertainment. These well-meaning officers proudly had taken their solemn oaths to serve and protect, but their actions and manner of professionalism mimicked the antics of the Keystone Cops. More often than not, they were stationed at the bottom of Circuit Avenue next to Giordano's restaurant, engaging in a feeble attempt to direct vehicle and pedestrian traffic, or patrolling the streets on foot.

These officers took great pride in enforcing the "rules of the road," which amounted to nothing more than ensuring that all vehicles stopped for pedestrians in a crosswalk. They sported

blue uniforms, clean and neatly pressed, with every acces-
sory—badge, belt with a holster, firearm, nightstick, flashlight,
whistle, and handcuffs—in its proper place. As kids, we used
to joke about whether they could actually handle a real-life law
enforcement challenge, such as a bank robbery or similar crime,
and concurred that, if such an event had taken place, they
would most likely have been the first to call out for assistance.

The excitement of downtown Oak Bluffs was magnetic to
teenagers, particularly at night. They gravitated to this small
area to hang out with each other and meet new friends, creating
an amount of activity unlike that found anywhere else on the
island. In addition to shops, restaurants, bars, and boutiques,
various other spots served as teenagers' social hubs. There they
found out who was on the island and what was happenin', long
before the advent of the Internet, cell phones, text messaging,
and countless other modern-day, techno-gadgets kids today
seem unable to do without. Back then, word of mouth and pay
phones were the only means of communicating.

Our crowd was a diverse mix of islanders and summer
residents, all of about the same age and with similar interests—
though various levels of maturity—trying to connect with each
other in the midst of establishing our own identities.

The Flying Horses was one of our favorite places to meet
because of its central location and its proximity to Circuit Avenue. Known for being the oldest running carousel in the country,
this indoor merry-go-round and arcade sat on a triangular piece
of real estate surrounded by streets on three sides. Patrons
entered through two doors on opposite sides of the old, wooden
building, and it was always crowded inside.

On most evenings, my friends and I sat on the steps leading up to the doorway. From there we observed hordes of people coming and going with children in tow, often waiting in line to ride the horses and try their luck at grabbing the brass ring. Tickets, candy, ice cream, soda, popcorn, peanuts, and cotton candy were sold at the tiny concession stand next to the carousel. The faces of little boys and girls, with chubby cheeks and big bright eyes, glowed with enchantment as they were strapped onto the backs of the colorful wooden horses adorned with manes and tails made from authentic horsehair.

A stocky, middle-aged man with salt-and-pepper hair and black-rimmed eyeglasses ran the establishment. He arrived early in the morning to open up and usually stayed long past closing time to sweep the floor and lock up the place. Throughout the day, he stood on the inside of the platform and forcefully manipulated the levers to operate the carousel.

In order to keep the accompanying music playing while the ride was in motion, he intermittently cranked the handle of an old, beat-up music box. The numbing music—a repetitious sequence of melodies that sounded as if it were played on an instrument mimicking a harpsichord—blended with the background noises of laughter, crying, talking, yelling, and the ringing of pinball machines also characteristic of this miniature amusement center.

In addition to his running the place, the old man had another job created by us kids, who kept him busy chasing us from the stairway so his customers could have unfettered access to the building.

"You kids can't sit here because you're blocking the doorway!" he often said with disgust.

We always moved when we were asked, only to return a few minutes later. This cat-and-mouse routine, which occurred almost daily, resembled scaring crows from a cornfield which they left only temporarily before flocking back to the same place. It got to a point where we would watch for him as we sat on the steps; this allowed us to anticipate his arrival at the doorway and abruptly leave before he was able to shoo us away. Although we teenagers got a kick out of playing this silly little game, his frustration with our immature behavior was clearly apparent.

A small booth wedged in one corner of the Flying Horses was where the ring dispenser was housed. A young boy, in his teens, kept the dispenser full for the duration of the ride. When he received a signal from the man in charge, the boy dropped a coveted brass ring into the dispenser for one of the lucky ring-grabbers to snag and win a free ride. When the ride was over, the patrons jumped off the carousel and the boy briskly walked around and collected the dispensed rings to replenish the supply for the next ride.

On the opposite side of the room, a variety of pinball machines and video games—including Ms. Pac-Man, Pong, and Galaxian—were lined up against a wall. This was where my friends and I spent most of our time and money while there. It was hard to resist the lure of the colorful flashing lights and melodic sound effects generated by the action of a metal pinball bouncing off the flippers and bumpers. To us, the thrill of being victorious over a pinball game was like hitting it big on a slot machine in Las Vegas; the only difference was that, instead of receiving a monetary prize, we won additional replays.

Directly across the street from the Flying Horses were Giordano's restaurant and the Clam Bar, two cash-only businesses owned by the same family for generations. Local favorites, the restaurant opened daily at 5:00 p.m. to customers standing in a line that often extended around the corner (no reservations accepted), and the Clam Bar opened midmorning and sold take-out fried seafood until eleven o'clock at night.

Several times a week, I strolled up to the counter of the Clam Bar to place an order for their crispy, golden French fries. After picking up my order, I immediately eyed the condiments on the countertop and, without having to think about it, generously sprinkled salt and doused vinegar on the fries before smothering them with ketchup. Satisfied that I had adequately seasoned them to suit my finicky taste, they were now ready for me to wolf down.

The hot fries in hand, my next stop was at the vending machine outside, into which I dropped fifteen cents to buy an ice-cold bottle of Fanta orange or grape soda. I sat on the curb in front of the Clam Bar, and, with great anticipation, satisfied my palate with the delicious fried food. That act was followed by long gulps of soda to wash it down.

Another popular teen haunt was the bowling alley on Circuit Avenue Extension—a side street off Oak Bluffs Avenue—right in back of the harbor. It was the only place on the Vineyard where you could bowl, but we rarely participated in the sport because it was always hot, dingy, and crowded inside. And, besides, my friends and I were just too cool to be caught throwing balls down an alley while sweating like a bunch of pigs. After all, being the proud teenagers we were, we had our illusionary reputations to maintain.

Instead, we chose to hang outside in front of the place and do absolutely nothing except kill time by watching people wander the streets. You couldn't find better entertainment anywhere—not even at a Barnum & Bailey circus—especially later in the evening when the barhoppers stumbled out of various watering holes in drunken stupors and attempted to navigate the streets in a conspicuously inconspicuous manner.

Not far from the bowling alley and the Flying Horses was Ocean Park, a large public garden that sat diagonally across the street from the Steamship Authority wharf. During the day, it was a beautiful oasis where day-trippers and tourists strolled through an open area of thick green grass and walking paths. People lounged on benches to enjoy the view of the gingerbread cottages along the street, the fountain pool in the middle of the park, and the bandstand and flower garden nearby.

But, when the sun went down and night crept in, this tranquil park morphed into a place that attracted all kinds of riffraff. A preferred hangout for teenagers, it served as a retreat from the noise and crowds only a couple of streets away.

Ocean Park provided my friends and me with a place to go after dark because it was an expansive area, illuminated only by sparsely placed light posts supporting dimly lit glass globes. There, under a veil of darkness, we engaged in illicit activities we never wanted to be caught doing, such as attempting to check out the anatomy of a girlfriend, smoking cigarettes, drinking cheap wine, or rolling a joint to toke some weed. If there happened to be too many people in the immediate vicinity, we always moved to a backup location, perhaps under the boardwalk at the wharf next to the ticket office, on the seawall between the wharf and the jetties, or on the jetties themselves.

The Inkwell, also known as Town Beach or Pay Beach decades ago, was a small public beach off Sea View Avenue and down the street from Ocean Park. This particular beach was where African Americans—as well as other ethnicities—went to enjoy a day of swimming and socializing.

For some reason, over time, it had become known as a "black" beach, but, as far as I was concerned, nothing could have been further from the truth—people of all colors, sizes, and persuasions went there. In fact, I first heard about it from one of my Portuguese friends who lived near my grandmother's house.

There were those who took every opportunity to use the Inkwell as their own personal soapbox to brag about who they were, who they knew, how affluent they claimed to be, or what they did for a living. But, to us, it was nothing more than just another place to go swimming that happened to be close to downtown. Not being concerned with superficial things such as social status or class, my friends and I came and went as we pleased, did our own thing, and enjoyed the colorful atmosphere indicative of this place. It was a hot spot, where diverse personalities intermingled during the endless summer days on the Vineyard.

Each time we left the Inkwell after an afternoon of swimming, our arms, legs, and faces always had turned an ashy gray from the residue of sea salt that had accumulated on our skin. With

sand-filled clothes and wet beach towels in hand, we crossed
Sea View Avenue and made our way through Waban Park—a
large open field of grass and weeds—where novice golfers
practiced their swings and putts in an attempt to perfect their
golfing skills.

This particular field was host to a variety of activities
throughout the summer, one of which included a display of
colorful Indian teepees intended to enlighten visitors about the
cultural aspects of Indian life on the island.

Quaint cottages surrounded the park, and it wasn't unusual
to see vacationers lounging on porches with a cool drink or
snack in hand as they soaked up the warm summer sun and
refreshing breezes that blew in from Nantucket Sound. A
friendly greeting, the wave of a hand, or a gentle smile was
exchanged with others as we passed by, and we were energized
as we continued our slow journey toward home.

After walking for another block, we followed the road to
the left at a fork, which brought us to Niantic Park—a popular place for tennis matches, basketball tournaments, and
impromptu pick-up games. Sometimes we sat on the bleacher
seats to watch a game or two, and, on occasion, we mustered up
the nerve to jump on to the court to compete with the legitimate basketball players. It didn't matter to us whether we were
on the winning team or not—we played for the sheer fun of
it—but we did usually come up with the short end of the stick
because we were no match for these accomplished athletes, and
we knew it.

Adjacent to the courts was a small playground with a set of
swings, a seesaw, a sandbox, and a slide, where young children

played for hours while their parents watched them or took part in a friendly game of tennis. Home was now only about a quarter mile away, so it didn't take long for us to get there after spending a day at the beach and making this last enjoyable stop along the way.

Chapter 21

House Parties

*A*mong the most popular social events for Vineyard teenagers were house parties. These informal gatherings featured curious boys and girls beginning to grapple with the challenges of adolescence. Those of us who needed an outlet for learning to walk the fine line necessary to avoid land mines disguised as estrogen and testosterone gone wild, found that these parties provided a means by which the concepts of attraction and sexuality could at least be explored—even if only in theory.

Not a week would go by without news snaking its way through the grapevine, of a house party being held somewhere in Oak Bluffs—in a yard, on a patio, in a garage, or in someone's living room. This would be another opportunity to show other kids just how cool (or immature) you were by throwing yourself out there and "strutting your stuff," sometimes at the risk of being ridiculed or sneered at by those older, more popular, more experienced, or all three.

What you chose to wear to a house party didn't really matter that much, which was fortunate for me because my clothing wasn't exactly off the racks of Louis of Boston, and they certainly didn't come anywhere close to what would be featured in *Gentlemen's Quarterly*. On the contrary, my wardrobe—if you could call it that—came from a makeshift clothing line that could have been named *Hand-Me-Down Duds*, *Patches Pride*, or *Tattered Tailors*.

I remember once being asked if the clothes I had on were hand-me-downs, most likely because none of them ever quite fit the way they were supposed to; they were too long, too short, too loose, too tight. Not wanting to be embarrassed, I vigorously denied it, knowing full well that the majority of my presentable clothes *were* handed down to me.

In an attempt to avoid that question again, I did my best to assemble an outfit of a decent pair of jeans not overly faded or wrinkled and a short-sleeved shirt with a collar. They were always accompanied by my only pair of worn-out, black leather shoes—complete with scuff marks, holes in the soles, and ground-down heels.

It was easy to find a party in Oak Bluffs by listening for the sound of scratchy 45 rpm vinyl records being played on a portable record player with a dull needle. Its tiny speaker was always pushed to the point of distortion because the only way you could hear it was to turn the volume all the way up. As the record player struggled to pump out R&B hits from Motown— James Brown, Kool & the Gang, Aretha Franklin, Sly and the Family Stone, and many other artists—you would notice that the fidelity was all high end, with no bottom. Have you ever listened to a Motown record being played without that deep heavy bass and the locking foot pedal pounding away at your chest? Believe me, it's just not the same.

The next thing you'd see were the tacky party lights, haphazardly strung from the ceiling if the party was inside, or snaked over hedges and through tree branches if it was in a yard or on a patio. The endless string of extension cords used to supply power to the lights most likely violated every electrical code in the book and, in all probability, was a fire hazard.

Modest refreshments—chips, popcorn, pretzels, peanuts, cookies, snack cakes, or perhaps some fruit piled onto small plastic plates—were set up on tables covered with thin, crepe paper tablecloths. We drank watered-down fruit punch or Tang, the drink of the astronauts. If the party was upscale by our standards, you might find assorted flavors of Popsicles being served, with soda or lemonade the beverages of choice.

Back in the day, a novelty product called black lights was used to create a psychedelic visual ambience that cast a greenish purple haze over everything. When you entered the room in grand fashion—your neatly picked afro glistening from an overapplication of Afro-Sheen and your wide bell-bottom jeans meticulously ironed and creased—the black lights stole the show by illuminating every speck of lint and dust in your hair or on your clothes. This made everyone laugh, and, as they did, their open mouths displayed sets of teeth that were a hideous monster green. The effect of the black lights converted those who wanted to talk into instant ventriloquists, as they attempted to speak without opening their mouths or moving their lips for fear of looking ridiculous. So much for the grand entrance.

The party usually began with the boys hanging out near the refreshments while the girls huddled together to see if anyone they might be interested in was there. The dance floor remained empty until someone got the nerve to ask someone else to dance. At that point, the party was on. It was akin to watching small groups of people standing around at the beach waiting for someone else to make a move because they didn't want to be the first one in the water.

As a teenager, I was shy and somewhat self-conscious. To protect my fragile ego (and to keep from making a complete ass of myself), I stayed on the sidelines and watched the more outgoing kids do their thing on the dance floor. You used to hear stories about how black people were born with natural rhythm. Well, God must have skipped over me when that attribute was handed out because my feeble attempts at "gettin' down" with the latest dance steps had me doing the Robot—twenty years before it ever became the name of a dance—my stiff, disjointed body jerking and twitching as if I were suffering from an epileptic seizure.

At one party, a friend of mine offered to give me a few pointers about coordination and how to move, but, as I quickly found out, you either had it or you didn't.

I didn't.

But, when a slow record such as "Love on a Two-Way Street" by the Moments or "Ooo Baby Baby" by Smokey Robinson & the Miracles was played, that presented an entirely different scenario. Then all you had to do was build up enough courage to ask one of the fine young girls of interest to slow dance. If you weren't immediately shot down, and she agreed to dance, you gently placed your arms around her waist, pulled her close to you, and slowly swayed from side to side.

After experiencing my first such dance, it became crystal clear why all the boys, as well as some of the girls, preferred slow dancing. In what could be described as a form of simulated intimacy—one of the many stops along the road to self-discovery—slow dancing facilitated actual physical contact between a boy and a girl. This naturally led to an increased heart rate, heavy breathing, and much sweating, all enough to cause an arousal capable of igniting the fires of Kundalini. This temporary state of bliss was short-circuited by a requirement only the boys could relate to—how to leave the dance floor when the song ended without looking as if you had a loaded gun in your pocket. This embarrassing situation made you walk with a slightly bent-over posture and forced you to retreat to any dark corner of the room until you could regain your composure.

It wasn't difficult to tell when a party had run its course or outlasted its intended duration. One definitive sign was the unmistakable glare from the parent or parents whose house or yard was being used for the party, followed by the look of disgust on the face of the boy or girl hosting the event when they were told that their guests had overstayed their welcome. All the food and drinks were long gone, and dirty paper cups, paper plates, and empty bottles and cans overflowed the trash barrels on to the floor.

Except for the most diehard partiers, the vast majority of the crowd had already left before the same records were played for the twentieth time. Stories, embellishments, and outright lies about who had gotten over with whom followed, and accounts were compared to see how many phone numbers and promises of future dates—real or imagined—had been collected.

House parties on the Vineyard gave teenagers a place to go at night in the safe environment of a burgeoning summer community—one that was instrumental in shaping our personalities as we transitioned from adolescence to young adulthood.

1963 Chevrolet Corvair

Chapter 22

First Car

*I*n 1970, I turned sixteen and a half (the legal age to operate a motor vehicle in Massachusetts) and received my license to drive. Not surprisingly, I couldn't wait to get my first struggle-buggy so I could cruise down to Woods Hole and board the ferry for a trip to the island.

To me, the only downside to being a newly licensed driver was that I was nearsighted and so had to wear corrective lenses. My goofy-looking eyeglasses were black, with old-fashioned granny frames that made me look like Catwoman from the *Batman* TV series. I was so embarrassed by those glasses, I refused to wear them in the presence of any of my friends. In fact, you wouldn't catch me dead wearing them. If I wanted to drive, however, I had no choice but to affix those hideous spectacles to my face.

Several months after getting my license, my sister-in-law, Jenny, helped me realize the dream of acquiring my first car. Because she was planning to buy a new vehicle at the time, she was kind enough to sell me her used car for the bargain basement price of one dollar. This dollar bought me a high-mileage, maroon-red, 1963 Chevrolet Corvair—not to be confused with the powerful and sporty Corvette.

The car was a two-door coupe with a four-speed manual transmission and a six-cylinder engine mounted in the rear. It was also equipped with dual carburetors and an independent suspension—which meant absolutely nothing to me as long as it started up when the ignition was turned on and moved when the gas pedal was depressed.

It didn't matter that Ralph Nader had classified it as being a deathtrap, or that my friends refused to ride around in the car with me. I had the freedom to come and go at will, which was a fair trade-off for the car's obvious lack of sex appeal.

For my listening pleasure, I complemented the in-dash AM radio with a cheap 8-track tape player, complete with a pair of tiny speakers that sat in the back window. In an attempt to compensate for the car's boxy appearance and conservative horsepower, I installed a glasspack muffler that was supposed to make the engine sound more powerful than it actually was. The only thing it did was create a loud, buzzing sound that resonated from the exhaust pipe. My presence in the neighborhood was no secret because the annoying sound of that muffler echoed between the houses and through the streets. This made it nearly impossible for me to approach the house in a stealthy fashion, putting a damper on my ability to sneak home, particularly after having stayed out until the wee hours of the morning.

Upon completing a series of crash-course lessons taught by my brother-in-law, Butch, on how to drive a standard shift, I was ready to hit the open road to embark on my maiden journey to the Vineyard—alone in my own car for the very first time. With a high level of confidence, I filled the gas tank and drove the car on to Route 93, which led to the Southeast Expressway.

It didn't take long for this novice driver—completely ignorant about traffic flows or the optimum time of day to drive to Cape Cod—to become gridlocked in the middle of rush hour traffic. The car crept along for miles as I alternated among the gas pedal, clutch, and brake, trying my best to avoid backing into the vehicle behind me.

Even with the windows rolled all the way down, prayers for relief from the stifling heat went unanswered; with each breath I took, the exhaust fumes and smog choked me and created a burning sensation in my lungs.

My blood pressure headed up and my breathing quickened as this harrowing, white-knuckle experience continued for about two hours—moving forward, stopping, waiting, inching up, rolling back, being honked at, cursed at, and cut off. Didn't any of the other drivers know I was an inexperienced, new motorist? That I was entitled to be treated with a measure of patience? Should they not have understood my plight and given me the right of way? Welcome to the wonderful world of licensed driving. These overly aggressive motorists easily lived up to their reputation of "Screw you buddy; me first."

The entire trip took four hours to complete—while shortening my life expectancy by several years. After finally making it to the ferry in Woods Hole, my left leg cramped up and felt as if it had swollen to ten times its normal size. My nerves were on edge from countless near-misses, and the terror of being among lunatic Massachusetts drivers—infamous for their rude driving habits—overwhelmed me. I drove down the hill to the staging area and got in line behind several other vehicles waiting for the ferry.

In an attempt to shake off the stiffness in my legs—I thought rigor mortis had set in—I stepped out of the car to stretch, before hobbling over to the ticket office to get the boarding pass for the car, a passenger ticket for myself, and a ferry schedule.

When I entered the white, rectangular building, a rotund, middle-aged man with silver gray hair was sitting on the other side of the counter. He seemed to be amused as he watched me walk off the spasms in my leg. Noticing him chuckling at me, I limped over to the window.

"Good afternoon. How can I help you today?" he asked.

"I'd like to buy a ticket for a car and one passenger," I said.

"Are you traveling to Martha's Vineyard or Nantucket?"

"Martha's Vineyard."

"One-way or round trip?"

"One-way. I'm not exactly sure when I'll be returning."

"Here you are, young man. The next ferry will be leaving at 7:30, so make sure you're back at your car by seven o'clock."

"Okay, thanks."

I paid the fee, grabbed the tickets, and left the building.

Soon after I returned to the car, the line of vehicles slowly began to move to board the ferry. After handing the tickets to a man on the ramp, I clutched the steering wheel and nervously inched my way onto the boat, being careful not to scrape the car against the steel wall or metal posts that separated the lanes of other vehicles already inside the ferry. Signs of other victim's mishaps were etched along the walls in the form of black marks and dents, indicative of the skill required to successfully maneuver a vehicle from one end of the ferry to the other.

First Car

On most trips to the Vineyard, I eagerly made my way to the upper deck to feel the spray of the ocean, breath in the fresh air, and enjoy the picturesque view while sailing across Vineyard Sound. But, this time, I sat in the driver's seat and lightly caressed the discolored black steering wheel as I admired my new car and visualized the roads to be traveled while on the island.

Looking down, I noticed a multitude of imperfections on the car—nicks and scratches on the windshield, cracks in the dashboard, worn seats, faded carpeting—all characteristic of the normal wear and tear to be found in an older vehicle. These things, however, did not dampen my spirits in the least. Instead, I quietly savored the moment as the teenager in me melted away, and, in its place, emerged the young man.

Forty minutes later, the ferry's diesel engines fell silent; we were almost there. The vessel slowly coasted toward the dock, and, as the two large doors to the freight deck were opened by crew members, bright rays of light from the setting sun filtered into the dark recesses of the boat. Standing on the ramp in front of us were two Steamship Authority workers waiting for the ferry to bounce gently against the wooden pilings as it snuggled into the slip.

Looking through the open doors, I saw throngs of people standing on the dock, eagerly awaiting the boat's arrival. After turning the key to the ignition to start the car, a wide grin spread across my face as I thought about the new chapter in my life about to unfold.

With great expectations, I motored off the ferry and headed for downtown Oak Bluffs without stopping at my grandmother's house. Eager to experience my first drive up Circuit Avenue, I went straight into town to see who was out and, hopefully, to be *seen* driving a car.

As usual, Circuit Avenue was clogged with a line of cars slowly creeping up the street. And, although my tired legs felt like wet spaghetti, I was more concerned about seeing if any of my friends were around.

My first pass around the block yielded nothing. It wasn't until the second time that I heard a voice yell from the sidewalk— music to my ears.

"Hey, Kevin, where'd you get the car?" asked Ritchie, one of my Vineyard coin diving friends.

I immediately pulled into a parking space and quickly removed my eyeglasses as he walked across the street and stood next to the car.

"What's going on, Ritchie? Check it out. I just bought this car for a buck," I said.

"You got this for only a buck? You've *got* to be kidding!"

"No, I'm not kidding. What do you think of it?"

"Snazzy little ride you've got there. How does it run?"

"Not bad. The only thing is that it's a stick shift and takes some getting used to."

"Hey, at least you're driving—which is more than I can say!"

"Where are you off to?" I asked.

"I got a job washing dishes at the Boston House. My break is almost over, and I've got to get back to work. I need to make that M-O-N-E-Y. You know how it is," he said.

First Car

"I sure do."

"Listen, we're all hanging out tonight after I get out of work. Why don't you meet us in front of the Flying Horses, say around 10:30?"

"I'll be there," I said.

"Okay, I'll see you then."

The time for my driving debut in front of my Vineyard friends was set. I left downtown and drove to my grandmother's house to let her know I was on the island and to drop off my suitcase. At ten o'clock, I jumped into my car and cruised back to town to meet up with my friends as planned. It was amazing how little time it took to get there driving, as compared to walking or riding a bike.

Within minutes, I was motoring down New York Avenue past the row of gingerbread cottages situated on the edge of the Campground, just beyond the Wesley Hotel. People were sitting on tiny porches, casually rocking back and forth while taking in the sights and sounds of downtown Oak Bluffs.

I took my foot off the gas pedal to slow the car down just before reaching Circuit Avenue. When I looked over at the Flying Horses and saw a few of my friends sitting on the steps waiting for the rest of us to arrive, in a foolish moment of vanity I snatched the eyeglasses from my face and tossed them on to the seat to avoid being seen in them.

My friends rose to their feet and started to cheer me on as they watched me drive by. This was my big moment. With a great sense of pride, I honked the horn and waved back at them—although they appeared as faint, fuzzy images even when I squinted—feeling like a king in a royal procession, acknowledging their presence and excitement for me and my towering achievement.

The Vineyard We Knew

As I drove on toward Ocean Park—my eyeglasses still on the seat—the road suddenly became dark and it became difficult to discern where I was going, especially with my vision blurred and out of focus.

I attempted to make a wide left turn to circle back around, but, while doing so, inadvertently crashed into the curbstone. After running the car up onto the sidewalk—flattening the two front tires—I shifted gear into neutral, engaged the parking brake, and got out to assess the extent of the damage. I looked at the punctured tires with disgust as the smell of burned rubber irritated my nasal passages. I was well aware just how much of a jackass I was to have ended up in this predicament.

With only one spare tire in the trunk, and knowing full well I needed two, I backed the crippled car off the sidewalk and parked it in a vacant space. The walk back to my grandmother's house was fraught with a torrent of self-lambasting and the use of a variety of colorful metaphors, during which I acknowledged the fact that I must have been suffering from an acute case of asshole-ism to have let this happen.

Early the next morning, I returned to the car and replaced one of the tires with the spare in the trunk; I carried the second tire to a gas station to be repaired. After it was patched, I rolled it back to the car and placed it on the wheel.

While tightening the last lug nut with the crowbar, I made a personal commitment to never again allow vanity to manipulate my actions to the point where my physical appearance took precedence over everything else. That was the moment I abandoned my silly pride and adopted a new attitude of "What you think of me is none of my business."

Chapter 23

Jungle Beach

*T*here were two unique beaches on Martha's Vineyard that attracted the attention of adventurous beachgoers throughout the 1960s and early '70s. Located about eighteen miles southwest of Oak Bluffs, they were beautiful and, in most ways, similar to other beaches on the Vineyard. However, they possessed a quality that didn't exist anywhere else on the island, a secret that eluded many tourists—one known only to the savvy or those who learned by word of mouth or happenstance.

The first of these beaches, in the town of Chilmark, was a secluded spot where hippies, baby boomers, and flower children gathered to enjoy an experience consistent with their belief in peace, love, and happiness for all humanity. The vernacular used in those days featured choice adjectives like "cool," "hip," "groovy," and "far-out." These words somehow took on an even deeper, cosmic meaning when uttered while under the influence of any number of mind-altering substances popular among the younger generation at the time.

The stunning beauty of Jungle Beach—an aptly named section of shoreline that was actually part of Lucy Vincent Beach—looked like Eden and was far off the beaten path. And it was popular with those who sought the freedom to shed their clothing and expose their nude bodies to public display.

Back then, few people knew the exact location of Jungle Beach. Most inquiries were answered with the statement that it was somewhere up-island, or near Chilmark, but, unless you were prone to navigating through paths of vegetation and underbrush, you would be hard-pressed to find it. Once you did, however, a whole new world opened up as you witnessed sights never before seen on a public beach in Massachusetts.

There, on crystal sands, the pristine ocean ebbing and flowing against the shore, were people of various ages and backgrounds walking the water's edge, swimming, sunbathing, and lounging—completely in the nude. They were free-spirited souls, uninhibited by embarrassment or shame and undaunted by any existing laws or ordinances against engaging in behavior that would be the hallmark of a nudist colony. It wasn't unusual to see individuals, couples, small groups of people, or even entire families taking part in this liberating portrait of life. You felt as if you were in a movie depicting a time long ago in a far-off, primitive land.

And no one gawked at each other or made a big deal about what was going on; here there was a unique understanding and acceptance of this behavior. Those who did not belong stood out like neon signs and were made to feel as if *they* were the ones who had the problem. Although difficult for the naysayers to understand, let alone embrace, nudity at this beach on Martha's Vineyard was as natural as eating or sleeping. It was a place where tolerance for one another was the most important thing—and the joy of youth was an everlasting utopia.

Not far from Jungle Beach was Moshup Trail, a narrow stretch of road parallel to the ocean. Abutting the lighthouse and cliffs at one end, this lonely lane wended through the peaceful town of Gay Head. On one side were dense areas of growth and thickets, separated by sandy paths that led to hidden, sparsely placed private residences. The opposite side was public, and featured small sand dunes covered with beach grass.

Snaking through this wide-open expanse of preserve land were long, winding paths of fine white sand that led to another beautiful beach. Moshup Beach, also known as Gay Head Beach, provided adventurous beachgoers with a viable alternative to Jungle Beach. This was noteworthy because Jungle Beach became inaccessible to the general public in the 1970s when its ownership was transferred to the town of Chilmark. As a result, its use was restricted to residents and guests of that town.

Consequently, people started using the outer reaches of Moshup Beach, just below the beautiful cliffs, for nude bathing. Countless times, I drove up-island to enjoy the serenity and the natural beauty of the cliffs and seashore. In addition to escaping from the chaos and congestion in Oak Bluffs, Vineyard Haven, and Edgartown, I found solitude there that enabled me to connect with my inner self and become one with nature.

While cruising around on a beautiful summer's day, absorbing the warmth from the sun and enjoying the invigorating ocean breezes wafting about, I gave some thought to where I might bring three of my friends from back home when they arrived the following day for a weekend of fun on the island. As I considered places that would be of interest, it occurred to me that the answer was on the very road I was traveling. Here was an opportunity to give them an experience they would never forget; I decided to take them to Jungle Beach.

The following morning, I left the house fifteen minutes before the ferry was scheduled to arrive and headed for the wharf in Vineyard Haven to meet my friends. It was the beginning of a glorious day of bright sunshine and a gentle wind that cleansed the air. Zipping down the road with the car windows open, I passed by a field of green grass and smelled fresh mint as I breathed in the crisp morning air. I was tickled with excitement at the thought of showing my guests around the island for the first time. To them, Martha's Vineyard was a mysterious place I disappeared to each summer; to me, it was an extension of my existence as a child.

When the ferry arrived, hordes of travelers disembarked with a sense of urgency, eager to begin their long-awaited vacations and leave the stress of their daily grinds behind. As the steady stream of passengers walking off the boat slowed to a trickle, I saw my three friends—Brian, Wayne, and Stephen—saunter down the ramp. Looking around as they stepped on to hallowed Vineyard soil, they spotted me waving to them from the ticket office and made their way through the crowd.

"What's happening, fellas? Welcome to the Vineyard!"

"Hey, man! What's going on?" Brian replied.

"Well, here we are; we have arrived!" Wayne said.

"Kevin, all I need to know is where the beach is," Stephen quipped.

"I thought you said this place wasn't crowded. That boat had so many people on it, I was afraid we were going to sink," Brian said.

"I told you more people visit the island on weekends than during the week. Now, stop your bitchin' and start having some fun. You all only have a couple of days and it goes by fast, so let's make the most of it," I said.

"He's right, you all. What do you suggest we do first?" Brian asked.

"Let's stop by the house and drop off your things. Then, we'll take a ride up-island to a beach I think you'll like."

"That sounds good to me. As you know, this is my first time on the island, so I'm open to just about anything," Wayne said.

Within an hour, we were on our way to Chilmark. The scenic drive over narrow country roads took us past forests, farms, and open fields where horses and sheep quietly grazed in green pastures. I could tell my guests were enamored by the beauty of the island as it unfolded before them, simply by the number of *oohs* and *aahs* they uttered as we cruised around various bends and up and down the hills. Finally, I pulled the car over to the side of the road and parked in front of a sandy path next to thick stands of underbrush.

"Okay, we're here," I said.

"Where are we?" they asked.

"At the beach I told you about when I picked you up."

"I don't see a beach. Where is it?" Brian asked.

"There is a beach here, but we'll have to do a bit of walking to get to it," I explained.

"I don't mind taking a short walk, but I wasn't expecting to be going on a safari," Stephen said.

"Come on. It will be worth it. Let's go," I said.

We got out of the car and began trudging down the path. During our minitrek, we stepped over boulders and waded through an assortment of vegetation, all while pushing aside low-hanging tree branches that obstructed the route. After walking for about ten minutes, we saw the dense foliage open up to a picturesque view of the ocean and a secluded beach where small waves gently washed onto the shore.

As we walked along the beach, tiny images of people appeared in the distance about a half mile away, and, when we got closer to them, my friends were visibly shocked by what they saw. Speechless at first, they soon realized their eyes were not deceiving them. Magically, their mouths became unfrozen and they were able once again to form words to express themselves.

"What the . . . ? I don't believe it. Check it out; those people don't have any clothes on!" Wayne said.

"Huh?"

"They're naked. All of them," Wayne said.

"Welcome to Jungle Beach. Just be cool; don't gawk, and try to act like it's no big deal," I said.

"I'll try, but I can't promise you anything," Brian said.

We continued to walk and eventually came upon a young black couple coming toward us, hand in hand. As their naked, sun-drenched bodies got closer, I noticed a certain familiarity about the woman. From a distance, her face began donning features I thought I knew from somewhere.

"Hey, that looks like—"

"It is. It's Elvira!" Brian said before I could finish.

"*Look* at her—butt naked and all," Stephen said.

She must have been just as stunned as we were because her eyes were fixed on us like a laser, and it wasn't because we had our clothes off—we didn't. But she and her boyfriend did, and there was no way out for them. In a shared moment of epiphany, we all realized we did, in fact, know each other.

The young woman was Elvira, the same Elvira who lived in West Medford and attended Medford High School with us. With no possible means of escape, she and her friend continued walking toward us, and we casually acknowledged each other as we passed by.

Although I told myself not to turn around and look, I couldn't resist the urge to catch a glimpse of Elvira's hot cross buns jiggling from side to side as she walked away. This was the first time I had ever seen a black person turn beet red from embarrassment.

Needless to say, my friends and I were beside ourselves with glee as we emphatically discussed the incredulousness of what we had just witnessed and how it would play out when we returned to school that fall.

We casually strolled along the entire length of the beach and back again, taking in the sights of this unusual environment in which we found ourselves.

"Isn't life strange?" I asked.

"What do you mean?" Wayne replied.

"I mean, young men spend every waking moment fantasizing about sex, drooling with desire to see a woman with her clothes off. Then, low and behold, not only does one come walking down the beach, but it's someone we know, from our own neighborhood. What are the odds of something like that happening?" I asked.

"At least a hundred million to one," Wayne replied.

"I would guess the number to be much greater than that—probably incalculable," I said.

"And you would most likely be correct," Brian agreed.

When I returned to school that fall, I happened to run into Elvira in the hallway. We exchanged greetings, briefly conveyed to each other how our summers went, and concurred about how disconcerting it was to be back at school.

Ever since the day I had seen Elvira and her friend sporting their birthday suits at Jungle Beach, I had often thought about how I would react when I saw her again. While conversing, I patiently waited for her to mention our impromptu meeting on the beach that day, but she never did, and neither did I.

Surprisingly, I heard of no rumors or embarrassing stories being circulated about the incident. Now, what were the odds of *that* happening? I would say that those odds were—infinite.

Chapter 24

Youth Center Gig

*I*n the 1970s, there was a Youth Center on State Road in Vineyard Haven, about two blocks from Five Corners.

Island teenagers converged on this small venue to escape temporarily their desolate off-season existence on the island. There weren't many options for young people on the Vineyard because just about everything shut down during the long, cold winter months. There were no jobs; tourism was all but dead; and businesses were boarded up with the exception of a few restaurants, a supermarket, a couple of gas stations, and a convenience store.

At the Youth Center, however, teenagers could hang out and play pool, table tennis, cards, watch TV, read, or simply vegetate. This popular place kept them off the streets where the temptation of mischievous behavior could easily have led them down a path toward juvenile delinquency. That old brick building served as an islandwide do-drop-in, and kids from all over the Vineyard got there any way they could—by car, bike, on foot, or even by hitchhiking—braving the frigid temperatures for the sole purpose of connecting with other teens.

Special events were held at the Youth Center on occasion, including some dances and performances by local talent. A couple of my Vineyard friends knew I was an aspiring musician back then, and one of them took it upon himself to speak to the management about having me and four other musicians from back home perform at a dance they were planning.

On a cold January evening, I received a phone call from a gentleman named Tom, the manager of the Youth Center at the time. He expressed an interest in having our five-piece R&B group, The Rightful Heirs, perform at their next dance. Our modest musical group was nothing more than a collaboration of a few friends from West Medford, each of whom began learning how to play his particular instrument only a few years prior. After discussing the feasibility of making the trip to the Vineyard among all the members of the band, we decided we would kindly oblige.

For the following two weeks, we hunkered down in a small basement a couple of doors from my house on Lincoln Street, and practiced various R&B hits of the day—songs we would attempt to play during our live performance. We were somewhat limited in our ability to recreate the lavish instrumentation and vocal arrangements found on many of the popular recordings, primarily because our group was really only a rhythm section of bass, guitar, drums, percussion, and vocals. What's more, we didn't have much experience performing in front of a live audience, except for a few local talent shows. Despite these constraints, we were determined to make the trip and put on a good show.

On a blustery Saturday morning, we met at
my friend Jackie's house to pack our old,
shoddy equipment—guitars, amplifiers,
drums, and a low-wattage public address
system—into a van for the trip to the Vineyard. Confident we were up for the challenge,
our entourage made its way to Woods Hole to
take the ferry to the island.

When we arrived at the Steamship Authority
dock, a deserted parking lot greeted us, a far cry
from the bustling tourist activity characteristic of
the summer months. Only three other cars were
waiting in line. The ground was frozen solid, and,
when I stepped out of the van, my shoes made a
crunching sound as thin sheets of ice broke, pierc-
ing the silence. I looked at the pier and noticed the
wooden pilings were topped with snow—resembling dollops of
whipped cream—as they rose out of the frigid waters where the
ferry docked.

"*Man*, it's cold!" Jackie said, as he shivered and blew into
his clasped hands to warm them up. "I hope my guitar stays in
tune, but I know these sub-zero temperatures are going to wreak
havoc on it."

"Yeah, it's so damn cold, the seagulls aren't even around. Now,
that's saying something," I replied.

"Let's take a walk down the street and get a cup of coffee
before the ferry comes in," Jackie suggested.

"We'll be right back. Does anyone else want a coffee?" I asked.

"Yeah, we all want one," they answered.

Jackie and I trotted down to the only restaurant open and returned with five coffees and a half-dozen donuts just as the ferry was being secured to the dock.

As I sat there sipping on my hot cup of black coffee, I looked over at the ferry and noticed it rocking from side to side while gale force winds and rip currents whipped it around as if it were a toy.

"I hope you all know how to swim," I said.

"What?"

"I *said*, I hope you guys can tread water," I repeated.

"Why would we need to do that?" Tony asked.

"Well, I'm looking at the ferry bobbing up and down, and, given how rough the water is, it made me think there just might be an iceberg or two floating around out there," I joked.

"Hey, man, don't be messing around like that. You *know* I can't swim," Paul said.

"I don't know about the rest of you, but *I* didn't come all the way down here to sink on a miniature version of the *Titanic*," Tony said.

"Relax. I was just kidding. Nothing's going to happen to the boat or any of us. Jackie and I have made this trip with our

families in weather much worse than this, and we're still around to talk about it," I said.

My words of encouragement provided little solace for two of the band members, who began to display signs of seasickness not long after we boarded the ferry. Their symptoms included dizziness, nausea, white knuckles, and a ghostly pale skin complexion. The boat lifted, dropped, and thrashed about for the entire trip across, as each wave tossed us around as if we were on an amusement ride. The usually talkative group didn't have much to say; they were preoccupied with trying to keep the contents of their stomachs down.

Upon reaching the Vineyard, we drove off the ferry and up the street to the Youth Center. Moments after turning on to a snow-covered driveway, a young man who appeared to be in his midtwenties opened the door to greet us.

"Hello, there. My name is Tom. Welcome to the island," he said.

"Hi, Tom; I'm Kevin. And these are the other members of the band. Meet Jackie, Tony, Paul, and Butch," I said.

"Hello, gentlemen. We're excited that you made the trip down to play for us. I've heard a lot about you and we're really looking forward to your performance. Let me show you where you'll be playing."

We followed him into the building and to a large room where he pointed to a makeshift stage area against one of the walls.

"Here's where you can set up your equipment. Let me know if there's anything else you need," he said.

"Okay. Thanks, Tom," I replied.

"Let's get the stuff out of the van," Jackie suggested.

We began lugging the equipment up a flight of stairs and through a side door, slipping and sliding on the icy surfaces as we went back and forth to the van. I grabbed hold of a metal handle attached to one of the speaker cabinets, and, because of the frigid temperatures, my fingers stuck to it as I strained to lift the cabinet through the door.

We made several trips back and forth to bring the musical equipment inside, and, one hour later, everything was in place and ready to go. To confirm that the gear was hooked up correctly, and to make sure our instruments worked, we ran down a couple of songs before anyone else was allowed to come in.

At six thirty sharp, the doors were opened and in they came. Teenagers from all over the island descended upon the Youth Center to check out these strangers from Medford who were going to be providing the music for the dance.

The five of us watched with amazement as kids filled every nook and cranny in the room, and we felt conflicting vibes of support and skepticism in the air. With the exception of a few of my Vineyard friends, no one else had a clue as to who we were. Even those who knew me—there to show support—had absolutely no idea of how well we could play or what we would sound like.

In a moment of camaraderie, the band members gave each other encouragement before taking the stage.

"Okay, gents. This is it . . . we're on," I said.

"Let's go kick some ass!" Jackie said.

We walked out and took our positions. I picked up my Fender

Youth Center Gig

Jazz Bass and secured it to my body by tossing the guitar strap over my shoulder and attaching it to the bottom of the instrument. After plugging in the cord, I flipped the switch to turn on my amplifier, then watched as the power tubes inside began to glow a warm, amber color. I was ready to play.

As I looked out at the crowd, it was difficult to see their faces because of the blinding stage lights shining in my eyes; the only images I saw were silhouettes. The sweet smell of incense filled the room, and a thin cloud of smoke gently floated through the air.

Out of nowhere, a nervous anxiety came over me. The fear of failure crept into my psyche, and self-imposed thoughts of doubt caused me to wonder if I was really up to the task. Will I play the right notes? Will I remember all the songs, their forms and tempos? My hands, though limber, began to perspire *and* turn ice-cold.

At seven o'clock, Tom stepped up to the microphone and introduced us with a warm welcome. We counted off our opening number and were on our way, musically speaking.

Jackie began strumming a chord progression in E minor as he depressed a wah-wah pedal with his foot. This was the introduction to the song "Who's Gonna Take the Weight" by Kool & the Gang, a tune we had practiced many times until we had gotten it just right.

Four measures later, I started plucking the A, open E, and D strings on my bass, producing a deep, rhythmic bass line that laid down the foundation for the song. Next, the drums and congas joined in, and, at that point, I became one with the music as it took control of my senses and flowed through me like a gurgling stream.

The Vineyard We Knew

The welcome sight of hands clapping and bodies swaying boosted our confidence as we immersed ourselves in the musical grooves we were creating. Before long, the dance floor was packed with teenagers two-stepping, bobbing, and shuffling to the music. Intermittent shouts emerged from the audience, prompting me to look up and see my friends cheering and waving their hands in approval. Sensing acceptance, our apprehension gradually diminished and we developed a rapport with the audience.

When the first set was over, we took a twenty-minute break to get some refreshments and review the list of songs we were going to play next. Encouraged by the kids' reaction during the first set, we rode a wave of positive energy, heightening our adrenaline level and setting the tone for the final set. We started to play again, this time, however, with more confidence and enthusiasm.

Then, halfway through the set's third song, the room went dark and our musical instruments went dead. A fuse in the antiquated electrical system of the building had blown.

The crowd let out a collective sigh of frustration as several adults scrambled to fix the problem. The only instruments now audible were the percussion, as Tony, Paul, and even our vocalist, Butch, with his tambourine, kept a syncopated rhythm going while the audience clapped along.

Within minutes, the power was restored and we picked up where we had left off. The outpouring of compliments we received from this young Vineyard audience made us feel like superstars on tour.

Youth Center Gig

However, reality has a way of humbling you and bringing you back to your senses. This was particularly true for us because we knew we still had to pack up the equipment and load it out in time to make the last boat back to the mainland. We had no roadies, but, fortunately, a few of my friends stuck around to help us move the gear back into the van.

After the equipment was loaded out and the lock on the door to the Youth Center secured, we said our good-byes, jumped into the van, and sped over to the dock just in time to board the ferry. Pleased by what we had accomplished, each of us quietly savored the moment as we gradually came down from the natural high.

Ironically, the cold, inclement weather to which we were so sensitive on the way to the island didn't seem to faze us in the least during the return trip. There were no fears of sinking to the bottom of the ocean or signs of seasickness—just subtle smiles of satisfaction, an admirable conclusion to a successful Vineyard concert performance.

I commended the guys for a job well done, and, as the ferry cut through the choppy waters of Vineyard Sound on its way back to Woods Hole, I thought, *there just might be something to this music thing.*

Tonight, the Vineyard; tomorrow—who knows?

Chapter 25

First Encounter

*I*t's not unusual to recall major events in our lives with laserlike clarity, for it is part of the human experience. From the moment we are born, to the time we expel our last breath, our brain miraculously records every nuance of thoughts, feelings, and emotions that are completely unique unto ourselves. As with snowflakes from the winter sky, so are no two individuals exactly the same. We develop and grow and learn to make decisions throughout life influenced by countless forces in the world—two of which are family and friends—sometimes for good, and sometimes not.

I remember meeting my very first friend when I was four years old and standing on the street in front of my house in West Medford, Massachusetts. I can also still feel how frightened I was as a five-year-old on the first day of kindergarten just before walking through the entrance to the Hervey School. In an instant, I can relive the frustration I grappled with at age six, sitting in a kitchen chair for hours trying to learn how to tie my shoes. And the joy that flowed through me as I kept my balance while riding a two-wheel bicycle for the first time. Through the window of my mind, I still see birthdays long past, holidays celebrated, and the excitement I felt when meeting new friends at elementary school, secondary school, and college—all fleeting moments of my own life's experiences.

Amazingly, I became aware of my sexuality when I was only five years old. Although I didn't understand it at the time, I learned that after I playfully climbed the pole that held up the Lincoln Street sign on the corner near my house, and slowly slid back down, I felt a sensation I had never felt before. All I knew was that it felt good—good enough to want to experience that feeling again. Even at that point in my fledgling life, I realized there must be a reason for my physical response to that innocent act, but I was much too young to comprehend or be concerned about such things.

I did, however, quickly move from being aroused by that inanimate object to becoming attracted to a girl named Abigail, who tickled my very young fancy when I first noticed her in kindergarten. In class, we were sometimes instructed to sit on towels spread on the floor and listen to stories or to sing along as our teacher, Miss Winn, played the piano. Not aware of the inappropriateness of my urges, I found myself wanting to sit as close as I could to Abigail—attempting to make bodily contact with her—to further experience that good feeling I found so fascinating.

It wasn't long before I learned what the birds and the bees were *really* all about, including the vacillating testosterone levels that wreaked havoc on my libido as I grew into adolescence.

First Encounter

My curiosity about the opposite sex became more prevalent as I got older, and the desire to experience the bliss of copulating was awakened from its latent state into something like a volcanic eruption.

>m

In 1970, my mother purchased a small cottage on Perkins Avenue in Oak Bluffs, directly behind my grandmother's house. This simple one-story structure—modest at best—had a tiny sitting area just inside the front door, a narrow kitchen, one bedroom, and a bathroom no bigger than a closet. Ma's long-range plan was to have it torn down so she could build a larger house to live in once she retired to the island. For several years prior to my mother's retirement, my grandmother kept an eye on the house while she vacationed at her own cottage during the summertime.

As we grew older and became more responsible, my mother allowed my brother and me to stay at her cottage for brief periods of time when we went to the island. This arrangement served a dual purpose, both providing us with some independence and also giving our grandmother a break from having to take care of us.

Our presence at my mother's place, however, did not deter Nana from making frequent rounds to scrutinize our behavior in a manner like that of a centurion patrolling his post. Notwithstanding the fact that our grandmother watched us like a hawk, it was there, in the small bedroom at the back of this cottage, where I lost my virginity on a warm and sultry summer's night at the tender age of seventeen.

The Vineyard We Knew

Her name was Elizabeth. She was a fine, slightly bowlegged girl with a spunky personality and golden blonde hair that fell midway down her back. Liz's eyes were mesmerizing—a deep blue with gray highlights—and could easily captivate you the moment you gazed into them. They had an uncanny ability to reach into your soul and spark your inner desire, like a powerful aphrodisiac.

Elizabeth lived in Oak Bluffs year round, about three blocks from my grandmother's house. We first met when we were just teenagers hanging out downtown with mutual friends. At the time, I didn't think much of her. She was just another pretty face, of which there were many between the locals and the hordes of tourists who traveled to and from the island throughout the summer.

But, as I began to see her more frequently—strolling down Circuit Avenue, at the Flying Horses, or swimming at Town Beach—I developed an irresistible physical attraction to her. And based on the subtle, flirtatious glances and body language she displayed toward me, I knew the feeling was mutual.

There was, however, one minor problem. Liz had a boyfriend who also lived in Oak Bluffs, and he was quite aware of the fact that I had my eyes on his girl. He knew I had taken a liking to her and would not hesitate to delve into more challenging pursuits if the opportunity ever presented itself.

For the remainder of that summer, Elizabeth and I engaged in our dalliance, getting to know each other better among the larger circle of friends we shared. We hung out at the Flying Horses, frolicked in the ocean at Town Beach, laughed, joked, and had fun in our own little world playing out in the eclectic town of Oak Bluffs. We talked about life and discussed mutual interests, including the fact that I enjoyed playing the bass guitar and she loved playing the drums. Female drummers back then were a rarity, so that made an instant impression on me.

⌒

That winter, I learned Liz had become pregnant and was expecting to give birth to her first child. The following summer, I saw her when I went down to the island. There she was—big stomach and all—going about her business, seemingly unaffected by the fact that she was a mother-in-waiting. Full of life and vibrant as ever, Liz never slowed down or stopped, and lived as much a normal life as possible, given the circumstances. So it was that we remained friends in spite of her transgression and the life-altering responsibility of having to care for a child.

When I visited the island the summer after her son was born, I ran into her downtown.

"Hey, Liz. How are you doing?" I asked.

"Fine," she replied.

"I heard you had a baby."

"That's right. A bouncing baby boy."

"Congratulations! That must be a trip—a new baby and all."

"Thanks; you have no idea how much."

At that point, I didn't know whether to keep talking about it because I detected a bit of uneasiness in her voice, so I changed the subject.

"Are any of the other crew on the island?" I asked.

"Yes. Cheryl, Mike, and Tim are down; I saw them yesterday," she said.

"That's cool. Maybe we can all hang out tonight if you can get out of the house."

Catching me totally off guard, Liz looked at me in a seductive way with her hypnotizing eyes—as only she could do—leaned over, and whispered, "I can."

It was apparent that the attraction was still there.

At that moment, conflicting thoughts filled my head as I weighed morality versus desire. After all, here was this girl to whom I was attracted who had a boyfriend and a brand new baby boy. And there I was, still a virgin. Because Liz had just become a new mother, she was light years ahead of me with respect to sexuality.

After collecting my thoughts, I responded by saying, "Good, I'll see you down by the Flying Horses tonight."

Later that afternoon, I went back to my mother's cottage where my brother, Chuck, was sitting in the kitchen talking with one of his friends from back home, Jimmy.

"What are you two doing tonight?" I asked.

"We're thinking of going into town for a while. Why? What are your plans?" Chuck asked.

"I have a date. Kind of."

"What do you mean, 'kind of'?"

"Well, I'm meeting Elizabeth at the Flying Horses."

"Elizabeth? You mean *the* Elizabeth?" he asked, with a devious smile.

"Yes, that's the one."

"Don't tell me my little brother is *finally* going to get some—"

"Get some what?" Nana asked as she waltzed into the house, peering at the three of us with suspicion.

"Get some ice cream," Chuck immediately replied.

"That's what I thought you were going to say. I stopped by to check on you all and make sure everything is all right," Nana said.

"Nana, everything is fine. We're all going downtown tonight; we'll be together so there's no need to worry," Chuck said.

"Okay, but don't stay out too late," she said, as she walked out the door.

"That's it. Come on, Jimmy, we're out of here; that's the tenth time she's come over to check on us in the last couple of hours," Chuck said, as he and Jimmy got up from the table and walked toward the front door.

"I'll catch up with you guys later," I said.

After changing into a clean pair of jeans—and contemplating the possibilities that might unfold that night—I got ready to hop in my car for the drive into town.

I arrived downtown at 8:30. First I stood on the corner of Circuit and Lake Avenues, nervously looking around to see if Liz had arrived. She hadn't.

Then I crossed the street and walked up the stairs to the Flying Horses to sit down and wait. There I attempted to block out the dissonant sounds of traffic and crowds as they converged into a convoluted chorus of white noise. As I gazed at the line of brake lights on cars slowly inching up Circuit Avenue, I felt a gentle nudge on my arm. I raised my head to look up and saw Liz's smiling face as she sat down beside me.

"Hey, you. I'm sorry I'm late. I couldn't get out of the house when I planned, but I'm here now," she said.

"Don't worry about it. The important thing is that you made it. You feel like going somewhere?" I asked.

"Sure. Let's get out of here," she said.

We left the Flying Horses and walked through the humid night air past Ocean Park, which led us down by the beach. Strolling along the shore, we noticed faint white lights glistening on boats in the distance as they cruised over the dark waters of Nantucket Sound.

It was close to eleven o'clock when we made our way back to the car and drove to my mother's place. We entered through the front door and saw Chuck and Jimmy sitting at the kitchen table, playing cards and listening to music.

"Hey, you all, what's happening? Liz, you remember my brother, Chuck, don't you?"

"Yes, I do. Hello. How are you, Chuck?" she said.

"Hey there, it's good to see you again, Liz."

"And this is his friend, Jimmy," I said.

"Hi, Jimmy."

"Hello," Jimmy answered.

"You two want a beer?" Chuck asked.

"Sure. Why not?" I said.

My brother went to the fridge, grabbed two bottles of Heineken, and placed them on the table.

"Thanks, Chuck," I said. "Hey, what's that you have there, Jimmy?"

"Acapulco Gold; good stuff," he answered, with a wide Cheshire cat grin. "Let me role a joint for you."

Jimmy took out a few buds of the gold-colored marijuana from a plastic baggie and removed the seeds and twigs from a clump. He broke the buds into fine flakes and carefully sprinkled them on to a thin sheet of E-Z Wider paper, which he rolled up with his fingers. After licking the glue to seal the edge, he handed me the joint. I placed it to my lips and lit it with a match. Inhaling deeply, I tasted the sweetness of the herb as it quickly went to my head, slightly disorienting me and causing me to become giddy. The joint was passed around among the four of us until only a small roach flickered in the ash tray before burning itself out.

Within minutes, the reefer took hold and I began to feel as if I were invincible. I could conquer just about anything.

I got up from the chair, took Liz by the hand, and led her to the bedroom in back. We sat down on the bed and embraced. In the dim light of a small table lamp, we took off our clothes and got into the bed. Not knowing exactly what to do, but with a heightened sense of arousal, I began lightly to caress Liz's soft skin with one hand, while attempting timidly to explore her voluptuous curves with the other.

After engaging in several minutes of what I later learned was foreplay, I could wait no longer. I haphazardly mounted her, albeit with a sense of purpose—as if I knew what I was doing—but, after some time spent with me awkwardly flailing around, she intervened and saved me from the embarrassment of my inexperience.

Entering this strange new world of physical bliss, I found myself entangled in a sexually choreographed dance as our bodies melded into one, leading up to the moment in which all perception of reality became distorted. Suddenly, every muscle in my body tightened at once—a prelude to reaching the climactic point of no return—and then I exploded with the force of a rocket blasting off its launching pad. Liz and I reenacted this enjoyable form of animalistic fornication until our bodies were completely drained of energy, after which we both fell asleep.

Very early the next morning, a faint ray of light appeared through the small bedroom window, abruptly awakening her.

"I have to get home," she said.

In a race to beat the rising sun, she got up out of the bed and quickly got dressed.

"I'll see you later on today," she said.

She then touched my hand and quietly stole out the door.

As I lay there, my mind still in a fog, I tried to comprehend the psychological and physiological transformation that had occurred within me, knowing full well that, as of that night, I was forever changed. While attempting to mentally reconstruct the images, sensations, and feelings of this new milestone in my life, I was slowly lulled back to sleep by the soothing melody of early morning songbirds.

It wasn't long before word got out that my once-platonic relationship with Liz had become quite physical. My so-called initiation into manhood gave me license to exude a level of self-confidence that had previously eluded me. In fact, my overly confident attitude quickly became an extreme form of cockiness.

Going forward, whenever we wanted to see each other, we had to duck and hide to conceal our rendezvous from her ex-boyfriend, who simply refused to give her up. And, although we tried to keep our involvement hidden from her stepfather, whose racial prejudice never permitted him to accept our interracial relationship, it was only a matter of time before he found out. This resulted in daily bouts of physical and verbal abuse, not only for Liz, but also her siblings and mother, all of whom lived under the constant threat of being thrown out of the house.

Always on the alert, we constantly looked over our shoulders when I picked her up after work or dropped her off down the street from her house to avoid potential confrontations. Add to that the staunch disapproval displayed by my mother when she learned about my involvement with Liz during a weekend trip to the island, and therein was a perfect scenario for a showdown between my mother and me.

"Who's this girl you've been running around with?" she asked.

"Her name is Elizabeth. She lives here in Oak Bluffs," I answered.

"Elizabeth? Is she white?"

"Yes, she is. Why should that matter?"

"It matters because she's white and you're black. You need to stick with your own kind," my mother said.

"Ma, it shouldn't matter. I should be able to see whoever I want. And besides, she's just a friend—"

"Yeah, right—a friend. You'd better watch yourself, young man. And don't be bringing any babies home to my house!" she said.

A deafening silence settled on the room as I tried to comprehend my mother's discontent.

"I heard this girl has a baby," she continued.

"That's right; she does. But it's not mine."

"Well, it better not be," she said.

"Ma, I know what I'm doing—"

"You know what you're doing? What the hell do you know? You're only seventeen and don't know a damn thing."

The Vineyard We Knew

It didn't take long for me to realize that trying to discuss this with her was an exercise in futility, so I bolted from the house and slammed the door behind me. Escaping from what I considered to be undue scrutiny, I trotted down a sandy road and purposely kicked up clouds of dust with each step I took.

Reflecting on what had just happened, my thoughts became erratic, and the anger within me rose to the boiling point. I was pissed off, and there was no denying it. Who was *she* to tell me what to do? My mother's disappointment didn't sway me in the least because it was already too late. The genie was out of the bottle, and there was *no way* I was going to stop seeing Liz. I was addicted to her—completely intoxicated by this new, sexual drug. Like a junkie in need of a fix, I would do just about anything to get it.

Both young, rebellious, and determined to get it on, Liz and I capitalized on the opportunity to do so in a variety of places, including in the privacy of my mother's cottage, on the open expanse of State Beach under the glow of a setting sun, and even within the claustrophobic confines of a car—wherever and whenever the chance to see each other presented itself. It was a long, hot summer, full of steamy trysts. My lust for her was insatiable . . . never quenched . . . always thirsting for more.

For the remainder of the summer, my relationship with Liz evolved. Then, throughout the fall, we kept in touch by way of correspondence and the occasional phone call when I had some spare change to use the pay phone. Most long-distance relationships are destined for failure, particularly when the participants are so young and so far apart, and ours was no different.

Well into the winter season I received an ominous letter

from Liz, requesting to meet me whenever I had the time and resources to make it down to the island. Having heard about "Dear John" letters, I tried to prepare myself as much as possible for what I was about to hear. Several weeks later, I made the trek down to the Vineyard in the dead of winter to confront the inevitable, face-to-face.

After arriving on the island on a cold and blustery afternoon, I walked over to Tuckernuck Avenue in Oak Bluffs—the place we had agreed to meet—adjacent to Waban Park. It was desolate and lifeless, a barren tundra, and, as I paced around and waited, a cutting wind blew relentlessly off the frigid ocean, numbing my face and hands and causing my nose to run. Having no tissues to wipe away the mucus streaming from my nose, I attempted to use the back of my glove to stop the flow, but to no avail. As I breathed in the cold air through my nose, I felt the oxygen crystallizing within my inflamed mucus membranes, and, each time I exhaled, I watched my hot breath condense into a cloud of vapor as it met the air and slowly drifted upward before disappearing from sight.

It was close to 2:30 when I saw Liz briskly walking toward me; her gait was that of someone on a mission. When she arrived, she greeted me with her warm smile, just as she always had done. On the one hand, she seemed happy to see me. But, on the other, it was clear that what she had to say was weighing heavily on her mind.

"Hi, Kevin," she said.

"Hey, Liz. How are you?" I asked.

"I'm not doing that great, but I'll be okay," she said.

"It sure is cold today," I said.

"Sure is. Listen, I know it took a lot for you to get down here, and I'm glad you could make it."

"What's going on?" I asked.

"There's been a lot going on, but I couldn't write it in a letter or say it over the phone. I wanted to tell you in person that I can't see you anymore," she said.

"Why is that?" I asked.

She looked at me with a serious expression on her face and attempted to explain the reasons behind this decision.

Liz had reached an impasse and now was compelled to convey her thoughts in a gentle but firm manner. I listened intently as she ran down a host of reasons why our puppy love relationship had to end. She explained that distance, motherhood, family pressures, and reconciliation with the father of her child were the primary reasons for calling it quits.

It was the first of many epiphanies I would experience throughout my life—defining moments that tested the true strength of my character.

Who was I kidding? I got kicked to the curb like an empty soda can tossed away after the drink had been consumed. And, as of that day, our relationship ended with a mutual understanding, an embrace, and a commitment always to remain friends.

Five years hence, Elizabeth and I unexpectedly crossed paths again. Perhaps it was coincidence, but I never believed in coincidence; my belief was rooted in knowing that all things that happen are destined to be. This time, however, our reunion of sorts was under completely different circumstances.

First Encounter

I was on tour with an R&B musical group called RHYTHM, and we were performing at a concert to promote our most recent record release. As I looked from the stage during the performance, I noticed the gaze of a familiar set of eyes peering out from the crowd. I knew those eyes; they were the same set of eyes that had swept me away during my first sexual experience—they belonged to Liz. Even though we had not seen each other for over five years, it seemed as if it were only yesterday.

After the gig, we went out for breakfast, and chatted, reminisced, and got caught up on how life was going for each of us. In the wee hours of the morning, she invited me to back her place, where we spent the night together, stoking again the fire that had burned once before.

That night mentally brought me back to when I was emotionally exposed and vulnerable. But, this time, my reaction was much different. Although I once again succumbed to her, I did so without really surrendering and was able to detach consciously and walk away afterward—unlike what had happened on the street next to Waban Park on that cold winter's day, five years before.

>⌒⌒

They say you always remember your first encounter, upon which the passage of time, distance, or life's experiences have no effect. Our brain, tirelessly working as designed, keeps observing, recording, and storing the unadulterated, unvarnished truth that can be recalled in an instant.

Perhaps that's why I can remember my first encounter with

Liz so vividly, and can do so with a smile—one borne of a unique kind of satisfaction that can only be realized through the balanced perspective of maturity. To me, it was an indisputable testament to the fact that I was no longer the shy, little boy I once was; because of Elizabeth, I had finally become a man.

Chapter 26

Lasting Impressions

*M*y grandmother cherished each day she spent at her house in Oak Bluffs—the same house in which she had summered for over forty years. Some of her favorite pastimes were gardening, sitting in the yard or on the front porch, entertaining friends, and taking care of her grandchildren when they were young.

While walking through the yard one afternoon, Nana inadvertently scraped her leg on the thorn of a plant growing among some bushes, which resulted in a wound that became infected. It never completely healed.

Carrie always had faith that any minor injury would take care of itself, and going to the doctor was not something done automatically. My grandmother's injury—and the fact that she was close to eighty years old—sealed her fate; that was to be the last summer she would spend on the island by herself. All visits thereafter were facilitated by Auntie and Uncle John, who brought her with them when they visited the island during the summer.

By this time, we grandkids no longer spent entire summers on Martha's Vineyard because we were older and working, attending college, starting families, and living our own lives. My mother continued to work but still had plans to retire to the island. Whenever possible, she made brief trips to the Vineyard to over-see the construction of a two-bedroom house to replace the small cottage she owned.

Ironically, now that my grandmother could no longer visit the Vineyard on her own, my mother checked on Nana's house when she went down—just as Nana used to do for Ma in years past—a seemingly natural reciprocal role reversal.

In the spring of 1984, my stepfather, John Hammonds, died of complications from emphysema in a hospital in Medford. One month later, Nana was admitted to another hospital in Boston where she remained for about a week, suffering from what was described as age-related health issues. In other words, she was preparing to go home to God.

My mother told me of a spiritual experience Nana had during her last days on earth. Nana was unaware that my stepfather had passed away the month before, and, when Ma and Auntie walked into her hospital room to visit, Nana's eyes widened and she became animated as she said, "John was here to see me last night."

"Who was here to see you?" my mother asked.

"John. John Hammonds was here last night. He stood there at the end of the bed and smiled at me," she said.

My mother and aunt glanced at each other, both clearly puzzled.

"Mom, you need to get some rest," Auntie said to her.

"I don't need any rest; I'm all right," Nana said.

My mother whispered to Auntie, "I think it's the medication."

"Could be," Auntie replied.

"Momma, we'll be back to see you tomorrow. Try to get some sleep, all right?" Ma said.

Nana shook her head and drifted off to sleep.

"We love you, Momma," they both said, as they kissed her on the forehead before leaving the room.

When my mother and my aunt returned the next day, the doctors informed them Nana was not faring well. Her frail body continued to weaken, and they did not expect her to survive much longer.

In a gesture of unconditional love, Ma and Auntie stayed with Nana until she left this life—quietly passing away at the ripe old age of eighty-nine.

Two years later, my mother retired to her newly constructed home on the island, just as she had planned.

Always the consummate individualist, Ma was adamant about maintaining her independence, and she protected it with vigilance. The eighteen years she spent on Martha's Vineyard allowed her to live the kind of life she wanted to live.

Because Ma was somewhat isolated from the rest of the world, I made it a priority to visit her as often as I could, particularly on special occasions, such as her birthday, Thanksgiving, Christmas Day, and Mother's Day. Whenever I walked through the back door and into the kitchen, Ma always had a big smile on her face. She was happy to see me.

"Hi, Ma. How are you?" I asked, as I gave her a peck on the cheek.

"I'm fine. How are you?"

"Everything is okay with me."

"Are you eating? You look like you're losing weight," she said.

My mother would have said that whether it was true or not, for she always looked for any reason to offer me something to eat.

"Ma, I'm not losing any weight. Come to think of it, I could probably stand to lose a few pounds," I said.

She looked at me and laughed in her high-pitched, melodic voice. "Kevin, you're crazy."

Bea had always been willing to prepare a hearty meal and break bread, but she did not get many chances to do so anymore because her children were all grown and it was just her, alone at the house on the Vineyard. My mother ate infrequently—just often enough to survive—but she felt useful when she had the opportunity to feed someone else.

"Are you hungry, Kev? Let me make you something to eat."

How could I say no to one of the few remaining joys she had in this life? Ma prepared her signature dishes like clockwork— the most popular being bacon, eggs, and grits, or pancakes for breakfast, a tuna sandwich and chips for lunch, and her delicious fried chicken, mashed potatoes, and a vegetable for dinner. I dare not forget her homemade apple pie for dessert, topped with a scoop of vanilla ice cream.

"Did you have enough? Would you like some more food?" she asked.

"Ma, please; I can't eat another bite," I said.

As always, you could never eat enough as far as Bea was concerned.

My mother went to great lengths to avoid the slightest appearance of monopolizing my time when I was on the Vineyard, regardless of the fact that the reason for my visit was to spend time with her. We often took leisurely drives around the island and reminisced about the good ol' days, when things were better. The air smelled cleaner, the sky was bluer, the sun seemed brighter, and, in general, life was good.

Ma and I began most of our outings by grabbing a sandwich to go at Linda Jean's in Oak Bluffs, or perhaps a cup of coffee and a muffin from the Black Dog Tavern in Vineyard Haven. During the course of our travels, we stopped along the way to indulge in an ice cream cone or pick up some fried clams—which she loved—and we never failed to stop by Alley's General Store in West Tisbury, a small country store that sold just about anything you could imagine. A sign hanging outside the store read "DEALERS IN ALMOST EVERYTHING," and Alley's more than lived up to that claim.

My mother and I watched many sunsets together, and we absorbed each precious moment of basking in the beauty of the warm yellow orb as it sank below the horizon at Menemsha Harbor. We thoroughly enjoyed the many wonders of nature that made being on the Vineyard that much more special.

Bea encouraged me to go out and do the things I loved to do while on the island, such as swimming, taking strolls, going into town, driving up-island, resting, or doing absolutely nothing if that's what I chose to do. My mother valued her independence, but I often wondered if she ever felt lonely on the island, particularly during the long, cold winter months. Ma didn't have an outgoing personality; she was quiet and reclusive. And within the small circle of acquaintances she socialized with in Oak Bluffs, only two were her true, close friends.

During my visits to see her, Beatrice bubbled over with joy, but she sometimes found it difficult to hide her sadness when it was time for me to go. I always saw it in her eyes. After saying our good-byes, I headed out the door, only to look back and see Ma sitting on the seat just below the bay window in her living room, watching me as I left the house to catch the ferry home.

There were times when Ma made the trip back to West Medford to visit, but she rarely stayed for more than a couple of days. Not wanting to overstay her welcome, Bea was always itching to get back home to the Vineyard; it was almost as if she were being pulled back to the island by an invisible but powerful force. Although she had been deeply rooted in West Medford for almost forty years, it was clear that Oak Bluffs was now her home. My mother belonged on the Vineyard—the last place she would live on her own.

In the years that followed, Bea lived in quiet solitude on the island. I frequently spoke with her on the telephone to check on her and make sure that she was all right.

One day, during a conversation, Ma told me she was starting to forget things; she couldn't find everyday items she otherwise wouldn't have had to think about. When it took her over three hours to find her way home from downtown one morning—a trip she had made a thousand times—she became alarmed.

Increasingly, her short-term memory began to falter and this posed a challenge to her independent way of life. It even got to a point where she thought someone was breaking into her house and taking things, not realizing she couldn't remember where she had left them.

"Kev, there's some really spooky shit going on down here," she said.

"What do you mean, Ma?"

"Someone has been coming into my house and taking things."

"Ma, I don't think anyone is coming into your house."

"Don't tell me; I know things are missing."

"What things are missing?"

"Someone's taking dishes, my socks, and my medications."

"Ma, who would want your medications?"

"I don't know, but I can't find them. Do you think I should call the police?" she asked.

"No, I don't think that's necessary, Ma. I'll be down this weekend and we'll try to sort this out together, okay?"

"All right, but I'm still nervous about all this," she said.

I did my best to reassure her that no one was breaking in and taking her things, but she was convinced otherwise. Over time, Ma began to display the subtle signs of neurosis, and she grew increasingly fearful of being in her house alone. Finally, my siblings and I decided an intervention was necessary, so I took her to a doctor to be evaluated. The test results revealed that my mother was suffering from a degenerative form of dementia—a precursor to the onset of Alzheimer's disease.

The Vineyard We Knew

Initially, it was devastating to come to grips with what was happening to Ma because she had always made her own decisions and taken care of herself. The prospect of having to leave the island was unsettling for her, but, in time, she came to terms with the fact that it was inevitable. My mother faced her illness with dignity and grace; she even joked about it, saying she didn't have a brain anymore—likening herself to the Scarecrow in *The Wizard of Oz*.

Eventually, my siblings and I made arrangements for her to move to an independent living residence on Cape Cod, but, after four months, it was evident she was no longer self-sufficient enough to continue living independently. My mother's inability to acclimate to this new way of life, along with the progression of her illness, made it necessary to pursue an alternate course of action.

Ma stayed with my family for about a year, at which time my wife, Olivia, selflessly took a leave of absence from her job to provide the necessary hands-on care and attention. Olivia had a close bond with my mother, one that had begun decades before when she and I were just teenagers growing up in West Medford. Now Bea was fond of Olivia's daughter, Keyarah, who had the unique ability to get Ma to smile, even on the most challenging of days.

It was difficult to watch my mother's cognitive abilities deteriorate, especially because, physically, she was as strong as a horse. Mood swings of happiness one minute, followed by angry outbursts the next, were indicative of the debilitating effects of Alzheimer's disease. The love and compassion Olivia and I had for Ma gave us strength and helped us to remain resolute while we dealt with the challenges of caring for her.

It wasn't long, however, before we were advised by her doctor that caring for my mother at home would become impractical, if not impossible. She now required a level of care that only trained professionals could provide. After conducting a comprehensive search into where our mother could receive the best care, in October of 2007 we moved her to a facility in Atlanta, Georgia, one that specialized in caring for individuals with Alzheimer's. In the nine months she was there, Bea appeared to be comfortable. The staff was friendly and they tended to our mother's needs with gentle compassion. Family members who lived in the area often visited her, which made it less stressful for her.

In July of 2008, shortly after her eighty-sixth birthday, I received a phone call from my brother, who told me my mother had been taken to the hospital. A battery of tests was conducted, and it was discovered that her kidneys had shut down; she was in renal failure. My mother's prognosis was not good, and we were summoned to be with her as she prepared to transition from this life.

Two days after I arrived in Atlanta, Beatrice was moved to a hospice facility, where she passed away seven days later, on July 21.

Saturday, October 25, 2008, was a bright and unseasonably warm fall day in Oak Bluffs, Massachusetts. Wispy, fair-weather clouds floated against a crisp blue sky, and a stiff wind blew from the northeast, causing large waves to roll onto the beach in succession. It was one month into the off-season on

The Vineyard We Knew

Martha's Vineyard; the streets were quiet and I could actually hear my thoughts without being distracted by the sounds of summer that normally filled the air.

While standing on the front porch of an old Victorian house across the street from the ocean, I heard the muted sounds of people inside going about the business of preparing for the memorial service to pay homage to my mother, Beatrice. And, even as I focused my attention on the activity taking place inside the house, I looked out over the water and smiled as I thought about how Ma would have commented on how glorious this day was. My heart was heavy, but I felt a sense of comfort in knowing this day was for her. I could almost hear her voice whispering to me, telling me not to grieve for her because she was now at peace.

For the first time in decades, my Aunt Florence, cousins Charlene and Vincent, my brother Chuck, sisters Joanne and Deirdre, and I, were once again reunited on this wonderful island—the place we had spent so many summers together as children. Deacon Bruce Gibson, my brother's childhood friend and friend of the family, flew in from Albuquerque, New Mexico, to preside over the ceremony. Family members, friends, and acquaintances from near and far were about to converge on the Vineyard to pay their final respects to "Queen Bea."

Reflecting back on the day before, I remembered the happiness I had felt with the arrival of people I had not seen in decades. That evening, a wonderful gathering commenced; dinner was served and a rebonding of sorts took place. Accounts of individual lives, the progression of careers, and intriguing stories were exchanged as we attempted to condense almost forty years of living into one short weekend.

Lasting Impressions

It was a joyous time, as well as a somber one. Old but familiar feelings of elation and joy were clearly present, and the manner in which those feelings flowed throughout the house was surreal; it accentuated the happiness we felt to be with each other again. But intertwined within the fabric of this uplifting emotional experience were momentary bouts of sorrow that appeared without warning, and they drove home the fact that my mother was no longer among us, despite the irony that she was why we were all together again.

Throughout the evening, we nibbled on finger food, partook in libations, shared stories, laughed, joked, cried, and acknowledged the fragility of life, all while expressing gratitude for the blessings in our own lives. The hours passed, until finally, in anticipation of the memorial service set to take place the following day, people began to retire for the evening.

Then, late that night, a ferocious thunderstorm roared in from the ocean with winds that howled through the bones of the old Victorian home. The walls shook violently, and bedroom doors opened and closed at will. Those staying there felt as if they were in a haunted house.

The following morning brought with it an unusual calm; the sun was shining brightly, and the air was fresh and clean. Now family members wondered if the gale force winds from the previous night were part of a scary nightmare.

"I thought the house was going to be blown into the ocean," Vincent said.

"It was wild. It sounded like somebody was banging on a metal trash can cover," Charlene added.

"The constant howling of the wind sounded like a freight train rumbling down the tracks in the dead of night," Joanne said.

The Vineyard We Knew

The large, oceanfront house rented for the memorial is rich in history. The Overton House—as it was once called—used to be owned by Joe Overton, a political organizer from New York who regularly entertained and housed many of his friends there during summers. Some of those guests were at the pinnacle of the Civil Rights movement's leadership in the early 1960s, including Dr. Martin Luther King Jr., Malcolm X, Adam Clayton Powell Jr., and entertainer Harry Belafonte. The historical significance of the property was proudly displayed on a plaque outside at the front entrance.

On the morning of the memorial, several rows of folding chairs were neatly arranged in the living room at the front of the house. This particular room, adorned with refinished oak throughout, had a warm ambience. Tall bay windows, from the ceiling to the floor, displayed a panoramic view of the Atlantic Ocean across the street and provided a picturesque backdrop for the service.

Sitting on top of an oblong table was a framed picture of my mother, Beatrice. Next to her picture were several white candles to be lit by family members as part of the ceremony. Bouquets of fresh flowers were placed in each corner of the room, as last-minute details were finalized. Before long, family and friends entered the room and took their seats. It was heartening to see the extent to which Ma was loved and respected; not only was every seat occupied, but some guests had to stand in the back of the room.

The service commenced, and my brother and I thanked everyone for coming to the island, acknowledging the fact that some of them had traveled great distances to be there. Deacon Gibson offered a prayer of comfort to the family, and my sister-in-law, Jennifer Parham, sang a beautiful rendition of the Lord's Prayer. My mother's obituary was read and the eulogy was given. A candlelighting ceremony followed, and reflections on my mother's life were offered by family and friends. Here is an excerpt from what I said.

A Tribute to My Mother

While attempting to put some thoughts together as to what I would say to honor the life of my mother, I initially found myself at a loss for the appropriate words.
What do you say about an extraordinary woman who, throughout her entire adult life, put her children above all else?

How could one adequately convey the high principles and values she believed in that ultimately shaped the very fabric of her life?

What measure could be used to determine whether her life was, in fact, productive or successful?

The answer to these questions is not complex. An understanding can be gained by simply taking note of the wonderful legacy that my mother left us with.

Beatrice was a loving mother who never openly displayed her feelings, but she always showered us with unconditional love and support, regardless of our shortcomings. She was selfless in that she never failed to sacrifice for her children when necessary, and willingly gave more than she ever took for herself.

The Vineyard We Knew

My mother was independent and strong, and she did things in her own way. She was a bit of a loner who never followed the crowd, for she had a plan for this life and faithfully followed her plan, even in the face of the many challenges that came before her.

She was a forgiving mother who did not hesitate to reprimand you when you stepped out of line, but was also able to look beyond an issue, no matter how egregious the act.

Ma was not only devoted to her children, but also to those she loved and held dear. If you were fortunate enough to have been her friend, you knew that you had a friend for life.

Bea lived a humble life; she didn't care much for attention, and never thought it necessary to boast about any of her achievements. To her, they were simply "the right things to do."

Mother often stressed the importance of living below your means and planning for the future. She was a practical woman, as evidenced by her resolve to work the 3rd shift for many years at the Walter E. Fernald State School. I once asked her why she did this, and it wasn't until I was much older that I learned what the term "shift differential" meant. The point here is that my mother capitalized on every opportunity to earn a little extra income to support her family.

Though not overly religious, there was no doubt as to Ma's belief in God. Without fail, she gave thanks before eating a meal, and knelt in prayer before retiring to bed at night.

As I pay homage to my mother today, I give heartfelt thanks to God for the blessings of her life.

My mother, Beatrice, and me

My mother firmly believed it was the small things in life that made the biggest difference. Simple gestures of goodwill—a ride to the supermarket, an offer to tinker with something around the house that needed fixing, a token gift such as a potted plant, greeting card, or a bouquet of flowers—made a lasting impression on her. She didn't ask for much in return for her generosity; an acknowledgement was usually more than enough. Ma gave us all she possibly could, and, in return, asked only that we respect one another.

I will always cherish my mother and the loving relationship we had. A lifetime of memories shall remain permanently etched in my heart with love, respect, and admiration.

Chapter 27

Philosophy of Life

*A*s I look back at my life, I clearly see the juxtaposition of how things are viewed from the vantage point of an adult, as opposed to that which is seen through the innocent eyes of a child.

In my youth, I felt protected. The days were never-ending, and the prospect of a long and fruitful life was something I looked forward to. Back then, time seemed to stand still, and the concept of growing old was inconceivable; it was an evolution I thought would never happen to me, at least not any time soon.

In the blink of an eye—a fair measure of the time we spend here on earth—I fast-forward half a century and ask myself: where did all those years go? My cognitive abilities have matured to a point where I feel I have acquired a certain amount of wisdom; my physical body—bumped and bruised even while performing admirably throughout life—has, to my satisfaction, met the rigors of a meaningful existence on this planet.

While I admit I'm not as youthful or nimble as I once was,

and am perhaps a tick or two slower than I used to be, I nevertheless cherish each precious moment of life that remains, fully cognizant of each breath I take and every beat of my heart as it tirelessly pumps lifeblood through me.

With gratitude, I acknowledge my ability to handle life's peaks and valleys, and attribute that ability, in part, to my experiences on the Vineyard as a youngster—experiences that were a catalyst to my becoming the person I am today.

My family, and all they shared with me while growing up, strengthened my character. I have learned to keep a balanced perspective by not taking myself too seriously, enabling me to remain objective in the face of life's challenges.

Without hesitation, I roll up my sleeves to deal with the nuances of life. But, more importantly, I engage in deep reflection, and the calm of my inner self takes me to a place where nothing can disrupt the peace I have within. This keeps me grounded and able to make some sense of this often senseless world in which we live.

If given the opportunity to live my life all over again, there are some things I'd do differently, as well as others I would not. It has been said that patience is a virtue; I know I could have exercised more patience when dealing with others, all of whom were less than perfect, as am I. Whether they chose to conform to my beliefs and expectations is irrelevant, for I have no standing to judge them. I have come to realize that everyone is unique in their own way, with various attributes and timetables for learning life's lessons.

My tolerance for others could have been greater, for I now appreciate the amount that must have been employed on my behalf. And the true essence of generosity—the act of giving of oneself, without the expectation of receiving something in return, not just on special occasions such as birthdays or Christmas Day, but for all 365 days a year—is something I now seek to achieve with a greater sense of urgency and compassion.

Having empathy for what others must endure in their lives has new meaning for me, for you cannot truly understand another's plight until you have walked down that same path yourself. I welcome new opportunities to travel those paths of understanding and wisdom.

As I meander down the road of life on a path of my own choosing, I think of those who have gone before me, down the paths they had chosen for themselves.

And I hope, when my time here is over and the spark of life fades into eternity, I will have left something for those who follow after me as they pursue their own dreams, down paths of their choosing—paths that ultimately lead them to fulfilling their unique purposes in this world—their destiny.

The Gazebo

Epilogue

When my grandmother passed away in the spring of 1984, her house in Oak Bluffs was left to my Aunt Florence. For eight years afterward, Auntie and Uncle John spent time there during the summer months—up until July of 1992, when Uncle John died of a heart attack while at home working on his car.

In 1994, the old house was burned to the ground by arsonists during the off-season. The following week, the Town of Oak Bluffs razed the charred remnants, and the empty lot sat undeveloped for three years.

In time, I contacted my aunt to ask if she would be willing to sell the lot to me; my intention was to build another house where my grandmother's house had once stood. After purchasing the lot from my aunt, but before I was able to begin construction on a new house, the Town expressed an interest in acquiring the property for the purpose of building a new library to replace the antiquated one downtown on Circuit Avenue.

After months of negotiation about the disposition of the lot, we agreed to a land swap. Two years after the deal was consummated, construction of the new Oak Bluffs Library began, and, as part of the project, a gazebo was built on the grounds next to the library.

The Vineyard We Knew

Today, close to the gazebo, on the same land where my grand-mother's house once stood, is a bench dedicated to the memory of my mother, Beatrice, and my grandmother, Carrie.

This bench sits on what I consider to be hallowed ground—the land where I, and the rest of my family, spent decades of summers—where we lived and learned about the meaning of family, discipline, survival, tough love, respect, camaraderie, and self-discovery. The bench not only memorializes two out-standing matriarchs of our family, but also represents the selfless contributions each of them made to who I became. My mother and my grandmother laid the foundation upon which I stand today, and, because of that, I will forever be in their debt.

❧

My siblings, cousins, and I forged our own paths in life, and did so after having been influenced to some extent by the summers we spent together as children on Martha's Vineyard. Our experiences there did not hinder our ability to go out into the world and reach for our dreams—to actively pursue our lives' purposes.

In fact, those experiences were partly responsible for build-ing strength and character in each one of us. They taught us right from wrong, how to navigate around or through obsta-cles, when to watch each other's backs, and, most of all, to appreciate life and acknowledge not only its brevity, but also its fragility. We were raised to believe that nothing is unattain-able if you have faith in yourself and make an earnest attempt to succeed.

Throughout life, we learned that failure was not an option; it was merely a default position—the result of having given up. We were encouraged never to give up, no matter how steep the climb or insurmountable the challenge appeared to be. It was imparted to us that success in any endeavor requires one to make wise decisions along the way, and we learned how important it was to utilize effectively the elements of desire, force of will, and good timing to one's advantage. Only then, will the fruits of one's labor manifest themselves in physical form.

Although the Martha's Vineyard we knew as children was much different from what people experience today, rare nuggets from our time still exist there. They can be seen in the majesty of the clay cliffs that reach for the sky as they slowly melt back into the sea; they can be heard drifting in the winds that gently blow over tranquil shores; their sweet fragrances can be smelled wafting among the fields, forests, and meadows that dot the landscape; they can be tasted in the succulent fruits and vegetables that grow in fertile Vineyard soil; and, last but not least, they can be felt deep within the hearts and souls of all people, past and present, blessed to have experienced a love affair with the island of Martha's Vineyard.

These rare nuggets shall forever remain, patiently waiting for anyone determined enough to seek them out. All that is required is a willingness to invest the time it takes to find them—an investment guaranteed to be well worth the effort.

If you've never experienced the magic of Martha's Vineyard island, I invite you to discover your own bit of whimsical fantasy. If you've already been captured by its spell, I wish you many years of the joy and enchantment that can be felt only by being there.

No words can describe the Vineyard experience more succinctly than those spoken by the late Henry Beetle Hough, a longtime Vineyard resident, author, Pulitzer Prize–winning journalist, and former co-owner of the *Vineyard Gazette*, who often said:

"Martha's Vineyard . . . next stop? There isn't one."

Photo Credits

For permission to reprint the following photographs and images, acknowledgment is given to:

Selden Bacon. [*Islander* inbound to Vineyard Haven] cover image.

Florence Guess (8, 13); Vincent Guess (8, 13, 51); Dick Whitney (184,214)

The New Bedford, Woods Hole, Martha's Vineyard & Nantucket Steamship Authority, 1958 (51)

Woods Hole, Martha's Vineyard & Nantucket Steamship Authority, 1966 (51)

Courtesy of the *Boston Herald* – Photo of Children Being Bused to School in Boston (162)

The Miami Herald. Photo of sanitation worker Ben Jones. Memphis, TN. 1968. "I AM A MAN" Project: March 8, 2008. Artist: Carl Juste (staff) (162)

Marion S. Trikosko. Martin Luther King, Jr. & Malcolm X waiting for press conference. 26 March 1964. Library of Congress Prints and Photographs Division. ID cph.3d01847. 01 March 2011. (162)
http://www.loc.gov/pictures/item/92522562.

Victor Hugo King. John F. Kennedy motorcade, Dallas, Texas, Nov. 22, 1963. Library of Congress Prints and Photographs Division. ID cph.3c34844. 01 March 2011. (162)
http://www.loc.gov/pictures/item/2004676894.

National Archives and Records Administration of the U.S. Information Agency, Record Group 306. Rosa Parks with Dr. Martin Luther King, Jr. (ca. 1955). Wikimedia Commons "File:Rosaparks.jpg" 15 October 2010. (162)
http://www.en.wikipedia.org/wiki/File:Rosaparks.jpg.

Yoichi Okamoto. President Lyndon B. Johnson, Rev. Dr. Martin Luther King, Jr. A2133-10. LBJ Library and Museum. 18 March 1966. White House Photo Office Collection. 01 March 2011. (162)
http://www.lbjlibrary.org/collections/photo-archive.html.

Cecil Stoughton. President Lyndon B. Johnson signs the 1964 Civil Rights Act as Martin Luther King, Jr., others look on. 276-10-wh64. LBJ Library and Museum Photo. 02 July 1964. White House Photo Office Collection. 01 March 2011. (162)
http://www.lbjlibrary.org/collections/photo-archive.html.

Warren K. Leffler. Civil Rights March on Washington, D.C. / [WKL]. 28 August 1963. Library of Congress Prints and Photographs Division. ID ppmsca.03130. 01 March 2011. (162)
http://www.loc.gov/pictures/item/2003654395.

Ira Rosenberg. [Muhammad Ali, bust portrait] / World Journal Tribune Photo by Ira Rosenberg. 1967. Library of Congress Prints and Photographs Division. ID cph.3c15435. 01 March 2011. (162)
http://www.loc.gov/pictures/item/96500238.

[Official Portraits of the 1976 U.S. Supreme Court: Justice Thurgood Marshall] 28 January 1976. Library of Congress Prints and Photographs Division. ID cph.3b07878. 01 March 2011. (162)
http://www.loc.gov/pictures/item/2002721282.

Warren K. Leffler. D.C. riot. April '68 Aftermath. 08 April 1968. Library of Congress Prints and Photographs Division. ID ppmsca.04301. 01 March 2011. (162)
http://www.loc.gov/pictures/item/2003688168.

Herman Miller. Malcolm X at Queens Court / World Telegram and Sun photo by Herman Miller. 1964. Library of Congress Prints and

Photo Credits

Photographs Division. ID cph.3c19478. 01 March 2011. (162)
http://www.loc.gov/pictures/item/97519439.

Yoichi Okamoto. Robert F. Kennedy Cabinet Room Meeting, W482-25. LBJ Library and Museum. 28 January 1964. White House Photo Office Collection. 01 March 2011. (162) http://www.lbjlibrary.org/collections/photo-archive.html.

Abbie Rowe. John F. Kennedy Funeral Procession Leaves the White House. 25 November 1963. John Fitzgerald Kennedy Presidential Library and Museum, Boston, MA (162)

U.S. Information Agency Press and Publications Service (ca.1953 – ca.1978). Civil Rights March on Washington, D.C. Actors Sidney Poitier, Harry Belafonte, and Charlton Heston. 28 August 1963. NARA- ARC Identifier: 542061. 01 March 2011. (162) http://www.arcweb.archives.gov/arc/action/

Bob Sandberg. [Jackie Robinson in Brooklyn Dodgers uniform, swinging bat] 1954. Library of Congress Prints and Photographs Division – ID ppmsca.00047. 01 March 2011. (162) http://www.loc.gov/pictures/item/97518915.

U.S. Information Agency Press and Publications Service (ca. 1953 – ca. 1978). Photograph of Leaders at the Head of the Civil Rights March on Washington, D.C. 28 August 1963. NARA ID – 542002. 01 March 2011. (162) http://www.media.nara.gov/media/images/27/3/27-0268a.gif.

Peter Pettus. Civil Rights March from Selma to Montgomery, Alabama. 1965. Library of Congress Prints and Photographs Division – ID cph.3c33090. 01 March 2011. (162) http://www.loc.gov/pictures/resources/cph.3c33090/

South Africa *The Good News*. Nelson Mandela in Johannesburg, Gauteng. On 13 May 2008. 01 March 2011. (162) http://www.sa.goodnews.co.za.

Scanpix. Jimi Hendrix at the amusement park Grona Lund in Stockholm, Sweden, May 24, 1967. 01 March 2011. (162) http://www.e24.se/Lifestyle/prylar/rockhistorien-auktioneras-ut_1475445.e24.

Arietta Smith Fildi on LJP assignment. James Brown. 29 Jan 1972. Southerly Clubs of Stockholm, Sweden. 01 March 2011 (162) http://www.en.wikipedia.org/wiki/File:James_Brown_Tampa.jpg.

U.S. Information Agency Press and Publications Service (ca. 1953 – ca. 1978). Civil Rights March on Washington, D.C. [Entertainment: Vocalist Odetta] 08/28/1963. NARA – ARC Identifier: 542020. 02 March 2011. (162) http://www.arcweb.archives.gov/arc/action/

Parade of Klu Klux Klan Through Counties in Virginia. 18 March 1922. Library of Congress Prints and Photographs Division – ID cph.3b42416. 02 March 2011. (162) http://www.hdl.loc.gov/loc.pnp/cph.3b42416.

Scott Bauer. Blueberries. USDA-Agricultural Research Service. 02 March 2011. (140) http://www.ars.usda.gov/is/graphics/photos/

Flying Horses Carousel, Oak Bluffs, Massachusetts. ShareALike 3.0 Unported. 02 March 2011. (218) http://www.en.wikipedia.org/wiki/File:Flying_horses_carousel_sign.jpg

Scott Bauer. Small Farm near Ames, Iowa. Nov. 1997. USDA Agricultural Research Service. 02 March 2011. (179) http://www.ars.usda.gov/graphics/photos/nov97/K7862-1.htm.

Sfc. James K.F. Dung – Department of the Army /Department of Defense – Office of the Deputy of Staff for Operations. U.S. Army Audiovisual Center. (ca. 1974 – 05/15/1984) UH-1D helicopters airlift members of the 2nd Battalion, 14th Infantry Regiment from the Filhol Rubber Plantation area to a new staging area during Operation "Wahiawa," northeast of C Chi, Vietnam. 05/16/1966. U.S. National Archives and Records Administration. ARC Identifier: 530610. 03 March 2011. (162) http://www.gallery.pictoria.com/natf/ photo/?photo_name=530610%20%28111-C-CC34613%29

Bibliography

Haley, Alex. *The Autobiography of Malcolm X.* New York: Ballantine
Books, 1964.

Milhomme, Bill. How it began: Grand Illumination. The Martha's Vineyard Times Online. http://www.mvtimes.com/mar-
tha's-vineyard/news/2009/08/13/grand-illumination-night.php.
(13 Aug 2009).

Cooney, Michael J. Martha's Vineyard Revisited. The Naturist
Society. http://www.naturistsociety.com/magazine/detail.jsp=21.
(11 Jan 2010).

Whitney, Dick. Whitney Web Site: Martha's Vineyard – The
Whitney Family Vacation Spot for Over 100 Years! Oak Bluffs,
Martha's Vineyard. http://www.dickwhitney.net/MarthasVine-
yardOak Bluffs.html. (5 Aug 2010).

About the Author

Kevin Parham is an author and professional musician who spent summers on Martha's Vineyard for over fifty years. As a result, he knows the island as well as can anyone not born and raised there.

He grew up in West Medford, Massachusetts, and graduated from Medford High School before attending Salem State College where he earned a Bachelor of Science degree in Business Administration.

He has held management positions at IBM Corporation and Verizon Wireless and has appeared before a wide range of audiences as a performing artist and speaker.

As a bass player, he has worked with an array of talented musicians, vocalists, and musical groups and has traveled extensively throughout the United States and Canada.

Kevin currently resides in Plymouth, Massachusetts, with his wife, Olivia, and stepdaughter, Keyarah.